Manage Your Mindset

Manage Your Mindset

Maximize Your Power of Personal Choice

Janet Hanson

ROWMAN & LITTLEFIELD
Lanham • Boulder • New York • London

Published by Rowman & Littlefield
A wholly owned subsidiary of The Rowman & Littlefield Publishing Group, Inc.
4501 Forbes Boulevard, Suite 200, Lanham, Maryland 20706
www.rowman.com

Unit A, Whitacre Mews, 26-34 Stannary Street, London SE11 4AB

British Library Cataloguing in Publication Information Available

Library of Congress Cataloging-in-Publication Data

978-1-4758-3572-4 (cloth : alk. paper)
978-1-4758-3573-1 (pbk. : alk. paper)
978-1-4758-3574-8 (electronic)

Printed in the United States of America

Contents

Preface

Have you ever thought that if you were smarter, or more gifted, you could achieve more? Do you sometimes wonder whether you are doing the best for yourself, for your children, students, employees, or others you lead? If you think about these things, then you are thinking about how to improve. You have begun a journey with this book to explore topics related to self-improvement. Yet what you will read is much more than that, because you are more than an isolated individual trying to figure out life on your own.

You are part of things both bigger and smaller than yourself. You are influenced by, and influence, others in small ways, in big ways, and in ways you may not have imagined. What you think and believe about yourself, and about those around you, matters. The journey through this book will help you explore why your beliefs about yourself and your world can limit what you see and do. You will find ways you can expand your focus and increase control of your choices. Strategies are provided to improve the accuracy of your evaluations of yourself and others. You can contribute to the development of yourself, your home, school, and world in ways that empower you and those around you to greater success.

There are many ways to go about reading this book. First, you can choose to enjoy the experience and read the book from start to finish, finding nuggets along the way that match your needs and expectations. Second, you can study the book, digging deeper into the references to advance your understanding of the topics. Third, you may choose to jump around the content and move to chapters that meet your current interest and needs, waiting to explore other topics at a later time. Or you can invite others to read along with you and develop meaningful learning together. No matter how you choose to approach reading this book, I hope you will enjoy the journey.

Acknowledgments

All accomplishments are a collective effort. The writing of this book was supported by the contribution of many minds and hearts to provide a message of hope with strategies for moving your goals forward along the path toward a bright tomorrow. David Gerhard, Karen Lillie, Gail Gerhard, and Bobbi Gerhard gave their time and talents to find ways to make the contents of this book flow smoothly for the reader. Aaron and Johanna, Chip, and Mary Rose, my dear children and many other of my immediate family members, especially my dear mother, Barbara, have been ever supportive and encouraging. How fortunate I am to have them all in my life! I also recognize the invaluable mentoring and advising I received from my doctoral committee chair, Dr. William Ruff, co-chair, Dr. Arthur Bangert, and committee members Dr. David Henderson, and Dr. Godfrey Sanders during my doctoral program at Montana State University, Bozeman. Our ongoing collaborations have contributed valuable supports for my development as a researcher and writer.

PUBLISHER'S ACKNOWLEDGMENTS

Grateful acknowledgment to the following professionals who reviewed or provided guidance during the writing of this work:

Andrea James-Rocha, MS, BCBA
Program Specialist/ABA
Garden Grove Unified School District
Garden Grove, California

Anita Henck, PhD
Dean, School of Education
Azusa Pacific University
Azusa, California

John Trent, PhD
Award-Winning Author
President and Founder of StrongFamilies.com
Scottsdale, Arizona

Chapter 1

Get Yourself Free—Manage Your Mindset

Not enjoyment, and not sorrow, is our destined end or way; but to act, that each to-morrow find us farther than to-day.

—Henry Wadsworth Longfellow, *A Psalm of Life*

A growth mindset can set you free from plaguing problems caused by a false belief that you cannot change. Everyone needs high skills, flexibility, and an accurate view of themselves and the world, in order to make choices that improve their experiences. A sense of well-being comes from having the ability to meet our goals and help those we love and lead. This book was written to help you manage your mindset, leading to increased power over your personal choices, so you can move farther along your chosen path.

Whether you improve, stay the same, or move backward is largely influenced by your mindset. Researchers, especially in the fields of psychology and marketing, have studied the concept of mindset for years. The results of the studies revealed that one's beliefs have tremendous influence on the ability to change old patterns, achieve one's goals, and adapt to new situations and changing circumstances.

The concept of mindset is framed in the theory of social cognitive learning (SCT). SCT describes learning as occurring through a combination of one's thoughts, feelings, and interactions with others (Bandura, 2001). How you experience your social interactions influences the sense of power you feel over shaping and controlling your world. The process of learning requires correcting the old ways you think and making new patterns.

Dr. Sternberg (2005), a researcher in the area of intelligence, wrote, "People who are the positive intellectual leaders of society have identified their strengths and weaknesses, and have found ways to work effectively within that pattern of abilities" (p. 190). Your understanding of your world is only

1

as accurate as your openness to change old patterns and respond to feedback. Your mindset belief about whether your intelligence is a fixed trait, or can grow, influences your openness to learn and vice versa.

Mindset is a term that has multiple uses in research and in popular use. In fact, if you search for synonyms of the word mindset, you will find several hundred. Most of the synonyms relate to abstract concepts of one's frame of mind. Examples of synonyms include the words *bias, attitude, expectation,* and *broad view*.

A review of antonyms, or words meaning the opposite of mindset can also help us understand the variety of uses for the term. For example, antonyms include *physical, deliberate, mindful,* and *knowledgeable*. By reviewing these synonyms and antonyms for mindset, we can develop a general picture that is fairly close to how mindset is described in the literature. Researchers use the term *mindset* as follows:

Mindset refers to the cognitive (or abstract mental) influences that relate to one's biases toward pursuit of long-term goals.

The opposite of *mindset,* then, would be the absence of a future orientation, such as thinking in the present (mindful), being physical, and avoiding bias in thinking. A common use of the term is to describe the way one views one's world. For example, the term *mindset* may be used to explain someone's bias toward a certain opinion about a topic, or life in general. This can be referred to as one's personal theory about a topic.

However, in common use, people often simply put a modifier in front of the word *mindset* and use the combination as a label to describe themselves. Labels describe fixed traits about a person, suggesting a predominant and enduring characteristic. For example, "I have a winner's mindset." Whichever way you view the meaning of the term *mindset,* the way you view your world influences what you see and the decisions you make.

The way you view the world includes previous assumptions and beliefs you have developed over time. This becomes your conceptual lens, the filter through which you see the world, just the way a lens on a camera can change the view. When your assumptions and skills are flexible, you can modify and adapt your behavior to be even more successful as the world changes around you and as you grow and experience new things.

WHY MINDSET IS IMPORTANT

An excellent analogy for understanding how important it is to have an accurate lens through which to develop skills is provided in a film from the PBS documentary series that shows navy pilots practicing jet aircraft landings on the *USS Nimitz* aircraft carrier in high seas. The following quote is from an officer on the ship describing the difficulties pilots have landing a jet aircraft on a pitching deck.

> Your brain, when you [approach the deck], you kind of start to think the runway is a fixed object and that's what you reference things on, where [in reality] it's not a fixed object and it's actually moving. It'll kill you in a second. You won't be the first one to fly into the water behind the ship. (Gibson, Davey, and Cotton, 2008, 3:00–3:39)

To us, the world can seem like a pitching deck. Our skills may not always be what is required for the task. The following sections discuss further why and how mindset works, why it matters, and how to manage your mindset to maximize your personal power to choose appropriate responses. Your ability to manage your mindset affects your ability to learn and grow.

BACKGROUND OF MINDSET

In her research, exploring students' approaches to learning, Dr. Carol Dweck (2008, 2010, 2015), of Stanford University, described the concepts of *fixed* and *growth* mindset. According to Dweck, a growth mindset is one's belief that personal traits are not fixed at birth but can change and grow through effort. She researched how students' mindset beliefs influenced their willingness to take academic risks and persist toward challenging goals, and even the type of learning goals they would choose (Blackwell, Trzesniewski, and Dweck, 2007; Farrington et al., 2012).

The concept of a *fixed mindset* can be compared to earlier theories suggesting one's behaviors come from innate qualities, or traits, imposed by nature at birth through hereditary influences. The concept of an individual fixed mindset belief compares favorably with the theory of nature versus nurture, popularized by Francis Galton (1874, 1889) in his works, *English Men of Science: Their Nature and Nurture and Natural Inheritance*. Galton proposed the evolution of traits and that intelligence was largely inherited. Galton was influenced by theories in Darwin's (1859) *Origin of Species*.

Similarly, a growth mindset belief has historical roots in theories by early philosophers. John Locke (1689), in his work titled *An Essay Concerning Human Understanding*, described a theory of mind as a *blank slate*, suggesting that individuals are born with an open ability to learn and are not restricted by hereditary predetermination (Nidditch, 1979). Though this is a very limited description, he highlighted the potential for human learning and growth.

HITTING A MOVING TARGET

As individuals, we need to be able to predict our world so we can control what we must do to protect ourselves and improve our situations. We want to become even better at providing for ourselves and those we love. We make judgments every day about why we and others do what we do. It is difficult to determine what is actually influencing our own behavior and those of others. Therefore, what can we do to improve the accuracy of our predictions?

The first way is to recognize that your beliefs about your ability to learn influence your judgments. Sometimes your worldview results in beliefs that become exaggerated fears, or the opposite, overconfidence. All humans are subject to similar systematic biases in their thinking that influence learning.

Many of our beliefs are the result of outdated information we remember, personal biases in the way we remember, biases developed from the news and other media, and a routine reliance on intuitions. One's intuitions may be built on inaccurate information if not regularly reviewed and corrected. Your judgments are influenced by your thought patterns, emotions, the context, and your personal priorities (Tversky and Kahneman, 1974).

Second, you can learn to manage your mindset, develop an integrated belief system, use more of the resources you have, and increase your flexibility. *Flexibility* is one's ability to respond successfully to the variety of new and challenging situations one faces in life. Creating a large set of skills, as well as developing a positive social network that provides feedback and support, is key to developing one's flexibility.

Deciding what to do in a given situation can be equivalent to landing a jet plane on a pitching aircraft carrier deck. Developing social skills to obtain help from others increases your potential for success and a growth mindset. For example, children were more likely to develop a growth mindset when they received positive feedback during their learning attempts, even though they failed (Claro, Paunesku, and Dweck, 2016; Dweck, 2016).

You can build growth mindset beliefs in yourself and in those you love and lead by responding with praise for effort and providing support when others experience challenges in life and in learning. Following is a brief review of the descriptions for the terms related to developing a growth mindset belief:

Beliefs are the confidence one puts in the truth or existence of something. When a person uses a belief to make decisions, he or she puts faith in the usefulness, or accuracy, of his or her judgment or perception. Your ability to choose actions that get good results is based on the accuracy of your beliefs.

Values are beliefs set in a hierarchy of importance. Values can be personal, developed from within, or transcendent, raising our understanding of our responsibilities beyond ourselves to our relationships with others. Our mind develops its own algorithms, or models, of how things work. Our mindset is a result of our personal algorithms such as core beliefs, expressed in language as assumptions and rules that drive our behavior.

Our personal algorithms develop from a variety of inputs over our lifetime such as our family system, culture of origin, faith group, peers, media, and educational system. Our models for how to act may not be known to us on a conscious level without the work of deep self-reflection and supportive mentoring. We must develop discipline to explore and reconcile our internal world with our external world. Supported self-reflection is a critical element of human maturity.

Science and mathematics have been developed to increase the reliability of data we collect and the validity of our conclusions. Language is often abstract and full of underlying assumptions. Mathematics has been used to test and explore reality through the development of "algorithms," or representations, "which [are] much more precise than that of ordinary language" (von Bertalanffy, 1968, p. 24).

Researchers often find it difficult to accurately measure what is truly motivating people's behaviors, what values they hold. More than one value may be motivating one's behaviors and choices. One's values can conflict with one another. Further, one's current situation, or social context, has tremendous power over one's ability to act on one's values. In fact, our values can be overridden as the primary influence on our behaviors.

Context cues, the images, environmental stimuli, and the structure of the system in which we work and live, can influence the choices we make. Internal and external pressures may interfere with our ability to act in integrity with our personal values. How can we tell whether a person promoting world peace, global warming, or animal rights is motivated by the desire to look good, to gain social approval, or if the person holds a true belief in the value of the cause?

One's individual behaviors related to achievement and relationships with others in power and authority are especially sensitive to multiple motivating influences. We often misunderstand the motivations for our choices and actions. Consider if you have ever violated your own principles when asked to perform a task under the authority of another or if you have experienced conflict from two competing values. Have you violated a personal value to meet the expectations of someone else?

We seek to protect self-image, sometimes overclaim our abilities or performance, or overrely on the accuracy of our assumptions. We make up stories to explain our behaviors and choices and sometimes reduce our functioning as a result. One way to correct errors in our judgments and redirect our actions is through the use of transcendent moral referents.

Researchers have identified a variety of common moral referents found across cultures and time. Some argued that there are inherent conflicts between individuals and cultures in the area of morals. The philosophical questions arising are impossible to reconcile because philosophies cannot be distilled to measurable, standardized universal constructs for predicting behaviors (Roberts, 1998; Stewart, 2007). Abstract concepts, such as values, are unseen influences on our judgments.

Similarly, *traits* are labels given to perceptions of enduring dispositions, occurring naturally, and are judged to influence behavior, attitudes, and one's motivation to persist. Traits are related to effort (Parks and Guay, 2012). The term *trait* suggests inflexibility, a lack of ability to respond, or adapt, and an inability to change when the situation warrants change.

How do traits and values explain the differences between fixed and growth mindsets? If a person has a high value for learning and a growth mindset, his or her self-image is not bound in a trait-based belief of intelligence. However, if you view a growth mindset as a trait, you may be thinking of it differently from the research. Some consider a growth mindset as similar to the definition of the personal *trait* called grit. "Grit is perseverance and passion for long-term goals" (Duckworth, Peterson, Matthews, and Kelly, 2007, p. 1087).

How does growth mindset differ from grit? Keep reflecting on how traits and values differ and how these terms are used when discussing a growth mindset concept. You will read how having a growth mindset can increase one's ability to reflect, adapt, and respond effectively to life's challenges (Dai and Cromley, 2014).

SHIFTING YOUR FOCUS

Though we have described mindset beliefs as either fixed or growth, one's mindset can shift between the two extremes along a continuum in response to different contexts and situations. In our daily experiences, we make choices on where to focus our mind. As complex social beings, we are constantly challenged with conflicting demands, so managing our mindsets by developing flexibility improves our ability to shift our mental focus.

When we focus intently, we selectively receive specific feedback from our environment, from feelings in our body, from others around us, and from our thoughts and memories. When our focus is narrowed, we increase our attention to just what we expect, or want to see, hear, and remember. Intense focus blocks out seeing what else is present in our environment.

Have you ever noticed that when you have an interest in something new, like buying a particular new car, you start seeing that model more often? This is an example of a widening of your focus from what you were previously thinking about and then a new narrowing of your focus to the interest in that model of car. We narrow our focus because we want to find ways to support our decision.

The narrowing of focus is adaptive and is *just a part* of the learning process. We use the input from our experiences to find patterns that can be repeated, as Longfellow wrote, to help us go farther along our path, toward our goals, today than we were before. We can improve ourselves by creating a more accurate view of our world and improving our ability to learn by understanding how our mindset influences our judgments.

Growth mindsets don't just happen. Do you believe you have traits that are fixed so you can't grow and learn, or do you believe that you can grow and learn through your own effort? Get a blank piece of paper and write your current understanding of what a growth mindset means to you. Label your definition, as a judgment about a *trait* you have or whether your mindset is a *value* that influences how you choose to act.

Do not worry about being right or wrong. We are exploring ideas and meanings together. Personal *reflection* will become a part of this journey.

Key points to remember

- *Mindset* is used in many different ways and is often described as either fixed or growth. When developed, a growth mindset belief can contribute to one's ability to be flexible in developing a more accurate understanding of the world.
- In general, *mindset* refers to the unique ways individuals use their thinking to anticipate and predict their world, and is influenced by the social context.
- Learning how to manage one's mindset can help one develop flexible skills and empower one's personal choice to engage.
- The power of personal choice helps one adapt to new situations, manage stressful life conditions, and resolve conflicts while being consistent with one's personal values and goals.

Chapter 2

Your Mind Is What You Make It

A mind is like a parachute. It doesn't work if it is not open.

—Frank Zappa

We make up stories about our experiences based on our feelings. Our feelings are the result of judgments about our experiences and vice versa. Your mindset, as your personal view of the world, influences how you remember experiences. Bandura (1989b) wrote, "Human memory is an active constructive process in which information is semantically elaborated, transformed, and reorganized into meaning" (p. 733).

In this chapter, you will read about the process of memory creation and how it contributes to learning. There are many different types of learning. The processes we use to create and correct our memories determine *the type of learning* we develop. Understanding how you learn and the different types of learning gives you increasing control over how you choose to apply your focus and take control of your learning.

HOW FOCUS INFLUENCES LEARNING

As humans, we have limited abilities. Even at our best, we develop mental representations of our experiences that often result from a limited range of focus. Our interests and goals determine where we put our attention. When we focus intently on one thing, we exclude data not considered relevant to the goal. Our focus may vary from what others are interested in, and this situation of *divergent focus* often occurs in classrooms, at home, and in the workplace.

For example, students' goals may vary from the classroom goals set by the teacher, or employees may have different goals from those of the company. Do you think when a student's behaviors lack focus it is because of the student's *traits*? Could off-task student behaviors sometimes be the result of *divergent focus* caused by divergent goals? Could the varied levels of individual skills students bring to the classroom, or negative emotional memories, cause them to have divergent focus?

Consider the use of labels, as traits, for students, such as attention deficit hyperactivity disorder (ADHD). Researchers have found that some students labeled with ADHD have experienced significantly more adverse catastrophic events (ACEs) in their lives than the average. The learning a student develops from experiencing ACEs can interrupt the student's ability to focus on school work (Burke Harris, 2015).

Students with a high need to find a safe environment may not be able to focus on the classroom goals set for them. Researchers have developed mindset interventions that support a students' sense of safety and build psychosocial skills that promote a choice to engage in academic behaviors. There will be a later section on *mindset interventions* that can be used to support productive student learning and increase students' choice to focus in the classroom context.

MINDSET AND LEARNING

The accuracy and quality of our learning is directly related to how skilled we are at reflecting, understanding our biases, and correcting errors and inaccuracies in our prior learning. Everyone is involved in learning, and because there are different processes used in learning, there are different definitions of learning that result. This section develops a framework for how to understand the different ways we learn and how mindset is intricately involved.

To be successful in adapting to the challenges we meet, we need accurate and sufficient input and skills to analyze and process our experiences. If we aren't open to correcting mistakes or adding to prior learning, we may stay stuck and be unable to grow and learn new things. Before we begin, it will be useful to define the difference between inputs as data, how we make sense of the input as information, and the processes used for creating new knowledge and skills.

Definitions

Data is the input we receive through our senses that create feelings and images in the mind, and are used in the development of memories.

Data becomes information when an individual gives meaning to the data by comparing his or her perceptions to prior memory. For example, if you once were burned on a stove, your memory says, "Don't touch a hot stove." That is information. You may not remember the details of the event though you will probably remember the feeling.

Memory—People store information in their brain, through chemical and physical processes, as images and feelings. Our memories become information for future use. When accessed from memory, this becomes new data in the creation of new information. For example, suppose a child riding a bike tries to jump it over a curb and crashes. He or she learns and will use his or her memory from the event when riding the bike in the future.

Memory provides information without conscious specific details, such as analyzing the curb height or other detailed data about the event.

Process of developing memory—We remember events as consolidated collections of data from our experiences and the meaning we have given them. We move data into memory as information once we give it meaning. The information stored in memory may be limited representations of one's experiences due to cultural biases framed by language labels, assumptions, emotional content, and inaccurate or missing data.

Biases—You create biases when you connect new experiences with prior stored information and emotional memories. Not all bias is bad. Bias has both positive and negative influences on our performance and judgments.

Skill development—After you order the data into memory, as information, you then arrange it in ways for future use. This process can be described and understood through the framework of skill theory (Fischer, 1980; Fischer and Yan, 2002).

Skill theory explains that learning occurs when people give meaning to their perceptions and organize these meanings into patterns, or skills. These skills will be available in the future as *behaviors*. Individuals develop skills in the hope these skills will give them success in new situations where they need to take action. Productive learning requires repetition, through practice, providing the brain opportunity to find patterns (develop skills) and correct errors (Fischer and Rose, 1996).

For example, developing interpersonal skills will help you decide after meeting a new person whether it is safe and beneficial for you to meet with him or her again in the future. Your decision is dependent on the way you evaluated the data you received.

A common use of the word *learning* refers to one's practice of storing data, such as school work, into memory and then demonstrating the ability to recall the data as information. Learning is an imprecise activity, and much of what is described as learning, in the common usage, is really referring to the broad category of memory development. When we create memories, we also make up information to fill in what is missing. We create stories that match how we felt about the experience.

The process of memory creation is done subconsciously for the purpose of making meaning from our imperfect understanding of our experiences (Kahneman, 2011). It may be difficult to accept that no one is able to recall everything perfectly; that is, we store memories as unique subjective representations from the meaning we make. You can test the differences in one's personal meaning making by participating in an activity together with a friend or spouse. Then retell in detail your memory of the event to each other.

TYPES OF LEARNING

One's idea of "self" is also created, and constantly changing and evolving, from one's memories of one's experiences in the world. We can say that we develop our sense of self through the process of learning. For example, we develop a sense of inner and outer; self and other. As we grow and learn more skills, we become increasingly able and willing to let more of the "outer" and "other" become identified with how we see ourselves.

In situations where we are challenged, we have crossed a boundary and our sense of self is challenged or threatened. Learning to improve our ideas of self, and others, requires challenging our biases by comparing them with new information through a process of self-reflection (Akkerman and Bakker, 2011, p. 132). When we choose to inquire into new ways of being, we are engaging in learning.

Learning can be described as occurring through two general processes, based on whether the learning improves our ability to function, or reduces it: the two are *productive* and *regressive* learning.

Productive Learning

Productive learning is an increase in information available for recall in the memory and, when given meaning and developed into patterns, results in a greater potential for adapting one's behaviors in new situations. Productive learning

- adds to the knowledge that you can use to generate new skills;
- increases your ability to function in a complex social environment;
- advances one's abilities and skills to act successfully in the world;
- increases with a growth mindset.

Productive learning focuses on the *potential for an improvement* in one's ability to reach one's goals. This type of learning helps one develop constructive beliefs, and put them in order of importance, in a way that guides the individual's choices and decisions. The more productive learning one has, the more choices of behaviors/or skills are available to use when responding to new situations.

There are two categories of productive learning: *receptive* and *transformative*.

Receptive learning refers to the memory stored as feelings and mental pictures, and is developed from the experiences we have in the world. By definition, receptive learning

- is the beginning process of changing data into information and then into knowledge and skills;
- is a mixture of facts, evaluations, judgments, guesses, emotional states, and feedback developed at the time the learning occurs;
- does not require self-reflection;
- can be active or passive.

During the process of *receptive learning,* information is placed in hierarchies in the memory. Memorizing school facts and being able to complete a test is an example of how receptive knowledge is used. Learning new skills such as driving a car or playing a piano, performing complex mathematical calculations, and performing a song are all examples of productive receptive learning. Receptive learning is framed in the context where the learning occurs.

An example of receptive learning follows. If a student wanted to earn high marks on a test, he or she might focus on reading the chapter and practicing answers to sample questions. The student may exclude distracting data from the environment by narrowing his or her focus to the assigned reading material, outlining, studying the class notes, and practicing recall of terms, resulting in a memory of the material.

Though the student's efforts may result in earning a good grade, a deeper exploration may reveal he or she still has a limited understanding of the overall structure of the concept or may lack the ability to apply the topic studied. The learning may or may not transfer to new situations.

Passive receptive learning occurs as the individual creates information inadvertently from input in the environment and places it into memory. Information and the knowledge one creates can be used productively or regressively. Everyone is subject to passive receptive learning. Passive learning may create negative emotions if one's experiences challenge one's sense of self or safety, or does not fit the mental representations the individual currently has built.

Active receptive learning requires personal choice to learn, that is, active inquiry. Motivation to learn can be described as occurring along a continuum from no motivation, to varying combinations of extrinsic (from without) and intrinsic (from within), to fully self-motivated.

Intrinsic motivation supports the learner's openness to compare his or her prior memories with the new experiences and make changes where necessary. Because this learning has meaning to the individual, it will more likely become transferable for use in new situations when mastered (Farrington, 2013; Novak, 2002; (Ponton and Rhea, 2006).

In the learning context, choice relates to the learner's power to make decisions and obtain the necessary resources to reach one's goals. Further, when individuals experience autonomy, they have greater personal agency, and this has been shown to result in greater health and sense of well-being.

> *Autonomy* differs from independent action in that autonomous action involves an alignment with the values embedded in the actions undertaken. An autonomous person takes initiative, feels an intrinsic sense of control, and feels the tasks performed have relevance to him or her. A sense of belonging and social identity with supportive others is inherent in the process . . . In contrast, independence is acting without help, support, or resources from others (Chirkov, Ryan, Kim, and Kaplan, 2003 in Hanson, 2017b, p. 45).

Mindset theory explains the learner's need for "establishing and maintaining . . . [a] subjective sense of prediction and control" over one's experience in the world (Plaks, Grant, and Dweck, 2005, p. 245). Don't worry, the concept of choice does not mean letting someone have unlimited free range over the classroom, work, or home environment to impose one's personal self-interest, or illegitimate goals (not considering all concerned).

Rather, *autonomy* is the preferred word to describe the type of actions one uses to develop productive learning. Personal choice to focus on learning in the classroom or workplace is not always a conscious decision. One's values, and the context where the learning takes place, influence where one focuses attention.

Extrinsic motivation places the learners sense of control outside of the self, and often results in rote learning. One's personal goals may differ significantly from the context goals. This process often occurs when the individual learner is responding to directions from others, to please others, or to protect one's self-image. In rote learning the individual learner does not challenge his or her existing knowledge structure (Novak, 2002).

Often students with fixed mindsets engage in rote learning and choose less challenging goals. An example of rote learning is when students work to earn As to prove their worth, or strictly to gain acceptance to a competitive placement, such as to a preferred university. What happens to students' mindsets if grades are viewed as currency to purchase self-esteem or entrance to competitive placements?

Conversely, an individual with a growth mindset, one who value's personal growth and enjoys learning, would more likely be willing to choose challenging goals, even after making mistakes. Educators, parents, and employers can support the development of individual growth mindsets in those they love and lead by providing healthy social supports that include recognizing effort and progress over time, rather than immediate results and an overemphasis on competitive accomplishments (Dweck, 2008; Farrington, 2013).

Regressive Learning

Some of our experiences may not result in what is defined as productive learning. Some learning may result in *reduced* functioning and contribute to poor judgments. If a person experiences a traumatic event, this can produce a response that fixes his or her learning into a protective behavioral response. One event can become an anchor that outweighs new experiences and reduces one's flexibility and functioning for years.

Regressive learning is described as the storing of experience into memory and an ordering of beliefs that create negative, fatalistic, fixed, or destructive meaning. This can result in behaviors that impair some aspect of the individual's functioning; and may have a negative impact on the group(s) in which the individual participates. Regressive learning reflects a fixed mindset and can be difficult to correct because of a lack of openness to change.

A fear response can occur when an individual experiences a real threat from an unsafe or unhealthy environment, internally, externally, or both; has few perceived choices to respond; and insufficient resources to overcome the threat. If one can't fight or flee, emotional withdrawal, denial, or habitual overreaction in new settings may be the alternative response. The learning reduces the person's ability to act productively in new situations.

For example, a woman shared that when she was a child, she saw a stranger peeking in the window at night. This experience created such a fear in her that she kept her window shades closed all through her life, even after she knew the threat was gone. On some level this person continued to recall the traumatic event and was protecting herself from the possibility it might happen again.

Overcoming Regressive Learning

Interestingly, not all individuals will regress from experiencing the same type of stressful situations. What causes one person to have negative learning and another to overcome and grow from a negative experience? A person's key personal values and the conditions existing in the social context can help prevent or overcome regressive learning. Individuals can learn skills to overcome regressive learning, but first the context of their environment must be addressed.

A limited context prevents us from seeing resources and influences that could change our perspective and help us learn and grow. Our stories influence our view of the world, what we see and feel. Excluding relevant information influences our stories. Our stories, as memories, are often made up after the fact (post facto) and conform to our feelings. Regressive memory is made up of stories we have for experiences that created negative feelings.

For example, if you watch a video clip of a man running up to another man in an alley and grabbing and pushing him, you might judge the first man's intentions as hostile and consider him a criminal, maybe a thief.

However, your judgment might change if you expanded the view of the situation and saw bricks falling off a scaffold overhead. How would you judge the man if you saw he was running to push the other man to safety and avoid his being hit by the bricks (Vucinic, 2005)?

A variety of strategies can help us correct our prior memories, such as being open to feedback and using self-reflection. The process is called *reframing* and it changes previous learning by physically altering the brain through natural means creating changes in consciousness.

One can experience personal growth and transformative learning with help from a supportive environment, instead of regressing and hiding from new experiences. Four essential skills are required for preventing, or overcoming, regressive learning:

- Proactively reaching out to others for help to reframe negative experiences and create a positive *shared meaning* of the experience(s)
- Developing an ability to *use words* effectively to communicate feelings
- A personal commitment to a set of *deep values*
- Skills for *adaptability*

The process of transformative learning to overcome regressive learning requires

- emotional stability;
- personal choice (autonomy) to put in the effort to reflect on one's experiences;
- a shift in one's choice of how to respond to the adverse event;
- creating a positive meaning for the event and a shift in one's self-image (Perry, 2004).

For example, if the woman who fears the loss of privacy chooses to self-reflect, she may recognize that she is older now and that she has spent years making good decisions that protected her from threat. She may be able to correct her feelings of helplessness by recognizing she has a strong support system and a safe environment. She could make positive meaning from the past experiences and choose to open her window blinds at appropriate times.

Putting in effort to overcome regressive learning can produce a broader, or transcendent, understanding of self, resulting in changes in one's mindset; how one views his or her world.

EMOTIONAL MEMORY

Much of regressive learning is emotional memory. One can always affirm one's feelings because there is no right or wrong in how you feel. Your feelings, however, contribute to your choices for action and vary based upon the ability to self-regulate. Your emotional state, the positive or negative feelings you experience, is not the reason you succeed or fail. Rather, the "essence of being human" is one's power to control one's self and improve one's quality of life, referred to as human agency (Bandura, 2001, p. 1, 1989c).

The amount of social support, self-control, and your ability to reflect on your own thinking influences the choices you make to express your feelings. Research suggests that the ways we express and manage our emotions are learned. Learning from our families' behaviors, the media, school environments, at work, and others may teach us appropriate, or inappropriate, means to express emotions.

Another type of learning, *transformative learning,* helps one overcome negative emotional memories and correct regressive learning by connecting with transcendent values that redefine one's self in relationship to others, the world, and transcendent forces influencing one's thoughts and emotions. This type of learning will be discussed further in the next chapter.

Key points to remember

- One's mindset, or worldview, is influenced by one's type of learning, and one's learning is influenced by one's mindset.
- This back-and-forth process can be understood as a reciprocal and continual process through which we can grow and change.
- Mindset is not an either "growth" or "fixed" concept. Mindset is a person's choice of how he or she views his or her world. Our mindset influences how we choose to respond to our world. We continually remake our beliefs in response to our thoughts, experiences, and feelings.
- A person demonstrating a fixed mindset response resists change and reflection, and a person using a growth mindset is more open to reflection and feedback.
- Flexibility in one's worldview allows healthy adaptation to the variety of circumstances one encounters and results from higher-order reflective thinking and transformative learning.

Chapter 3

Maximizing Your Power of Personal Choice

Three things shine before the world and cannot be hidden. They are the moon, the sun, and the truth.

—Pokala Lakshmi Narasu, *The Essence of Buddhism*

The concept of a growth mindset is a theory of the mind. A theory of mind "is the ability to know that different people have different knowledge about the situation and the ability to differentiate between what I know and what you know" (Lee, 2016, 4:22). This means that each person constructs his or her understanding of reality in different ways. Researchers found that a theory of mind can exist in children as young as two years old.

Two key abilities are necessary to function successfully in society. The first is a theory of mind, and the second is the ability to control the way one presents oneself in social situations. These two functions work together to develop a social identity, which is so critical for gaining others' trust and support (Lee, 2016). Developing a positive social identity and a sense of belonging also bolsters one's self-image (Ma, 2003).

When we feel safe, we don't have to do the emotional and psychological work of protecting our self-image from threats. This leaves us with mental energy in reserve to engage and develop new productive learning. Organizations show improvement when the individuals in them work to support the development of positive social identities in their members (Berber and Rofcanin, 2012; DiPaola and Tschannen-Moran, 2001; Hanson, Bangert, and Ruff, 2016; Hanson, Ruff, and Bangert, 2016).

An individual needs high skills to present his or her social self in a way that shows he or she recognizes others' perspectives and supports them. In doing so, one must still maintain a stable sense of self. Immature social development creates disruption in social settings when an individual has an excessive need to present his or her ideas and fails to recognize value in the uniqueness of others.

For example, the diagnoses of both attention deficit hyperactivity disorder and autism are associated with an individual's low abilities in presenting oneself socially and in recognizing others' unique ways of seeing the world, that is, lacks the development of a theory of mind (Lee, 2016). Effective social organization requires a willingness to acknowledge and value others and the ability to agree and work together toward common goals.

The higher one's level of ability (or power) to act in integrity with one's values through personal choice, the greater the potential for health in the individual and in organizations. *Ability* here refers to the development of all skills related to healthy functioning, not just IQ; as suggested in the following statement, "Intelligence is . . . a person's ability to adapt to the environment and to learn from experience" (Sternberg and Detterman (1986) in Sternberg, 2005, pg. 189: Weschler, 1943).

Individuals need to have flexibility in their priorities in order to integrate in social situations and to adapt to new circumstances, just as a jet pilot must be able to adjust the altitude of the plane at any moment when landing on an aircraft carrier's pitching deck. However, there are values that transcend time and place and do not change. These transcendent values help individuals improve their relationships with others through the development and recognition of a transcendent self-identity.

TRANSFORMATIVE LEARNING

Transformative learning (TL) provides the foundation of caring for ourselves and an understanding of our responsibilities in relationships with others and our world.

Brookfield (2012) in Katz (2013) explained basic beliefs underlying TL as follows:

> Belief in the ability to define oneself . . . learning from rational, emotional, imaginative, or spiritual experience either alone or in relation to others; and . . . understanding not only just how the world is, but also how it might be changed for the better. (p. 455)

Elias (1997) in Dirkx, Mezirow, and Cranton (2006) shared

> Transformative Learning is the expansion of consciousness through the transformation of world views and the specific capacities of the self: transformative learning is facilitated through consciously directed processes such as appreciatively accessing and receiving the symbolic contents of the unconsciousness and critically analyzing underlying premises. (p. 125)

Your belief in the potential for growth in yourself and others is important to the process of TL. TL helps individuals develop improved connections (human not digital) with others and form *transcendent* values. Transcendent values include caring for others, holding an awareness of the consequences of our actions as important, personal responsibility for managing one's own behaviors, and a productive ordering of one's beliefs, that is, conforming our behaviors to a "great exemplar" (Lewis, 2002, p. 701).

You have the potential to improve *your abilities and the functioning of others in your life through the process of TL.* TL includes the process of conscious reflection, that is, thinking about one's thinking. Not everyone realizes that a person can observe one's thinking in a detached and objective way that allows openness to consider other possibilities. Higher-order thinking allows one to connect to transcendent values, used as standards or guides.

REFLECTION

Reflection occurs through the mind's conscious awareness of the "self." Without a sense of self, one cannot self-reflect, so necessary for correcting errors in our thinking and developing self-control. *Self-reflection* is a recursive process that supports "the evolution of insight and the creation of new meaning" (Rossi and Cheek, 1994, p. 162). Recursive means that one is routinely called to reflect again after prior reflection and change occurs.

According to a saying attributed to Confucius, "By three methods we may learn wisdom: First, by reflection, which is noblest; second, by imitation, which is easiest; and third by experience, which is the bitterest" ("The Analects" as reported in *Chambers Dictionary of Quotations*, 1997, p. 279). One can use the tool of reflection to challenge accuracy in one's memories and to identify biases that systematically occur from the way one's mind processes input from the environment.

Reflection creates awareness of the personal and contextual influences on learning, and is useful because we don't automatically understand how to act appropriately in all social contexts. In addition to the use of reflection, we learn from others, through experiences such as modeling and feedback. Transformative learning differs from receptive learning by expanding one's awareness beyond the language processes used in the mind. Transformational leaders, with transformative learning, lift the group to higher levels of motivation and values.

In a fixed mindset, a person does not shift his or her beliefs through processes of reflection. In a growth mindset, the individual believes he or she can change. Therefore, the individual is more open to feedback. A growth mindset can be used to engage learning to improve errors in memory, correct judgments, and develop improved skills for controlling one's emotions, environment, and to adapt in new situations.

How and what we learn greatly contributes to the quality of our life and to reaching our potentials, both individually and collectively. The topic of mindset is intricately involved in the *quality and type of learning* you can achieve.

Caveat. Having a fixed mindset may be realistic in some settings. Being open and receptive to new learning requires a healthy and safe environment.

TRANSCENDENT REFERENTS PROVIDE POWER FOR INTEGRITY

Milgram (1974), a Harvard researcher, was motivated to perform experiments to understand how individuals developed the flexibility to act when their values were threatened. He replicated certain situational variables he felt were similar to those in World War II concentrations camps. He hoped to discover environmental or psychological conditions that might have contributed to normally ethical people performing horrific acts against helpless others.

Milgram designed an experiment in which each participant was asked to press levers on a machine that, he or she was told, would give increasingly higher levels of electrical shocks to an individual seated in another room. Researchers observed to see how far the participants would go in following directions of an authority figure when the participants believed they were harming another human being. The participants were not aware the machine in the experiment did not give actual shocks to anyone.

When participants administered what they thought were progressive levels of shocks, they heard a person in another room groan or and ask them to stop (actually it was a recording). Many participants became distressed during the experiment and expressed their unwillingness to continue. However, the majority of participants continued administering shocks against their stated better judgment, later explaining they did so because they were directed to continue by the experimenter.

In some cases, however, subjects had the personal agency to withdraw, in spite of directions to continue. What made the difference? The researcher explained the difference was the ability of those participants to act *autonomously* in the face of conflicting values. Recall autonomy means the ability to choose between independent action and social integration. The individuals who disobeyed the researcher withdrew from their social role as participant and acted independently.

The individuals with the ability to act autonomously often reported they were able to defy the directions of the experimenter because they referred to a transcendent moral reference, or spiritual authority. The internalization of a higher authority than the experimenter gave individuals a sense of accountability for their actions. They kept a sense of responsibility which gave them the power to behave in ways consistent with their values (autonomously).

In addition, the individuals were able to resolve internal conflicts caused by their situation. When an individual seeks to reduce internal conflict, he or she must first affirm a positive self-identity that is aligned with his or her personal values. Individuals who internalize a transcendent referent develop a transcendent sense of self.

Milgram suggested implications from his study. He explained that individuals using an external moral reference had a stronger identity than the social role they played in the experimental study. Milgram demonstrated human agency is influenced, not only by social situations, but also by unseen transcendent beliefs. Transformative learning requires a shift in one's values and a reevaluation of one's personal sense of self (O'Leary, 1998).

As previously stated, transformative learning helps one overcome regressive learning by connecting with transcendent values that redefine one's self in relationship to others, the world, and transcendent forces influencing one's thoughts and emotions. The following list provides elements of transformative learning:

- requires intrinsic, or personal, motivation to engage learning;
- requires openness to new data that may challenge previous understandings and assumptions;
- uses feedback and input from the social environment;
- requires referents outside of oneself (transcendent sources) that support making meaning in a new way;
- requires a change in one's sense of self to include ideas that transcend one's self;
- challenges the knowledge structure in one's memory through higher-order reflective thinking processes (thinking about one's thinking);
- increases content accuracy, corrects and creates awareness of systematic biases, helps avoid inaccurate assumptions and judgments;
- develops personal and contextualized meaning;
- increases one's flexibility, the ability to respond in complex social situations;
- contributes to improvements in one's functioning and has a positive impact on one's work or social group.

Key points to remember

- Theory of mind and the ability to control the way one presents oneself in social situations are key to successful social participation.
- The learner must actively choose to engage new learning and change prior mental maps, by repeated practice, in order to develop the ability to use the knowledge in new situations.
- A person can overcome regressive learning by developing a new self-identity and making positive meaning from a negative situation.
- Help from one's social group is important in overcoming fixed mindsets and in developing the ability to regulate one's emotions that result from negative experiences.
- Self-reflection, and reflection on transcendent referents, is necessary to develop transformative learning.

Chapter 4

Gain Control of Your Learning

The greatest obstacle to discovery is not ignorance—it is the illusion of knowledge.

—Daniel J. Boorstin, in Krucoff, 1984

Learning involves the creation of cognitive, emotional, and muscle memory. Mastering a new skill is like a routine of working out at the gym; building mental muscle by creating new neural associations. This requires repeated practice, over time, in a variety of contexts. Understanding how your brain operates during learning can create a baseline for building strategies for growth. This chapter explores ways you can take control of your learning by understanding what brain researchers have discovered about how we master new skills.

Researchers tested the brain responses of different individuals expressing either a fixed or growth mindset using new brain imaging techniques. The results suggested that those with growth mindsets had better self-monitoring, cognitive control, and awareness (improved focus) of their mistakes, and were able to develop more adaptive responses than those with fixed mindsets (Moser, Schroder, Heeter, Moran, 2011, p. 1488).

Each person has a unique (idiosyncratic) brain pattern, as memories, he or she creates during learning. New long-term memory develops when the brain's electrical circuitry connects across all regions, connecting the prefrontal cortex activity to both hemispheres of the brain. This same cycle must occur through iterations, repeating the learning in new contexts until a mapping occurs across the brain as a new skill.

MAPPING SKILLS TO THE BRAIN

Think of the mind as a unique tool for collecting, comparing, and analyzing experiences to create new meaning. Our thoughts, as ideas, are mapped onto the brain, which is then used to make decisions. Children first develop simple ideas of objects and then make connections, as relationships, between objects. Progressively, categories and systems of interrelationships are added. Simple ideas become complex mental maps of abstract ideas as we mature and grow (Baumeister, Masicampo, and Vohs, 2011).

Language develops to express and receive these ideas within one's culture of origin, placing differing priorities on various aspects of the social experience. Our language is a tool that also becomes a limitation because it is socially constructed and is unique between social contexts. This means our language may not include concepts other cultures value and vice versa.

Therefore, much of what is considered important is implicitly given to us through language. Our memories are state dependent (connected to our emotions) so a particular memory can be stored, as if "locked away," and become inaccessible when a person is in a different mental state ("Hypnosis and mental structure," n.d.). It is important for individuals to develop a broad range of skills by repeatedly participating in a variety of situations connected with positive emotions.

As Fischer (2006) explained:

> When faced with a situation that requires a new skill or understanding, a person gradually builds a complex skill to act in the situation, but it *readily collapses with changes in context, state, or goal* [italics added]. The person then rebuilds the skill again and again, producing growth curves that show [recurring broad arches]. The hierarchical complexity scale makes it possible to examine this process across tasks, domains, and people. (p. 28)

Rakic (1971, 1988) in Fischer (2006) adds:

> In living organisms, growth generally occurs through cycles. A prime example is the growth of the cortex [brain], which grows six layers in a cyclical process of neuron generation and migration. . . . A single growth process thus produces six distinct layers in which cells for different layers end up with vastly different functions, even though they are all created by the same process. (p. 2)

This process of brain development can be observed as one practices a new skill. As the learner progresses, his or her ability to demonstrate the new skill during practice moves from a chaotic pattern to a more regular pattern, and finally to a consistent demonstration of high-level skills. Figures 4.1–4.3 show the skill level attained during practice attempts for novice, intermediate, and expert performers while learning a task.

Figure 4.1. Graph of novice learner's ability to demonstrate a skill during practice attempts (unstable). *Source*: Adapted from Fischer, 2006, *Growth Curves for Learning a Task: Novice, Intermediate Performers, and Experts*, p. 39.

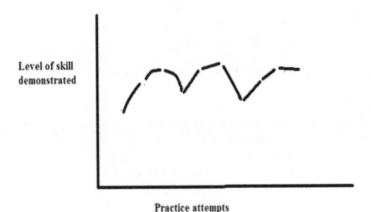

Figure 4.2. Graph of intermediate learner's ability to demonstrate accomplishment of a skill during practice attempts (stabilizing). *Source*: Adapted from Fischer, 2006, Growth Curves for Learning a Task: Novice, Intermediate Performers, and Experts, p. 39.

Another way of looking at how the brain moves through three levels of learning to develop mastery patterns is called quantum learning, described as

- serial thinking, linking neurons (novice);
- patterned thinking, across a neural network (intermediate);
- and whole brain thinking, neural connection throughout the whole brain (expert) (Zohar, 1997, in Vella, 2002, p. 73).

Practice attempts

Figure 4.3. Graph of expert's ability to demonstrate performance of a skill during practice attempts (stable). *Source:* **Adapted from Fischer, 2006,** *Growth Curves for Learning a Task: Novice, Intermediate Performers, and Experts,* **p. 39.**

Your dreams and daydreams are another way you attempt to create order, make sense of your experiences, and predict and control your world.

THE MIND-BODY-CELL CONNECTION

Think of your brain as a projector room where you create miniature movies out of all the data you receive from your senses and from bits and pieces of prior memories (movies) you created. These movies are your *stories*, or the individual theories you create about the world, the idea of self, and others around you through your experiences (Dweck, Chiu, and Hong, 1995). Your dreams and daydreams are another way you attempt to create order, make sense of your experiences, and predict and control your world.

You practice every day creating these stories. Challenges in your life push you to create new stories. The mind can be described as the storehouse, in subconscious memory, of ideas you develop from how you view the world through the senses (as stories, images, symbols, etc.). These memories are connected with the feelings (created by the hormones) at the time the learning occurs.

Memories are made up of chemicals that create patterns of transmission between brain cells (neurons). These chemicals are distributed throughout the body in tissues and cells in a mind-body-cell connection (Rossi and Cheek, 1994).

The mind-body-cell connection has been studied showing how the mind, through thought and feeling, encodes a physical map on the brain of the meanings given by the mind to experiences. These "mental maps" are influenced by our social context and culture through language and external input

(Ruff, 2002). Electrical, chemical, and physiological changes in the brain have a significant part in the processing of data into information and its storage as memory.

Prediction and Decision Making for Action

One's mindset is part of a mental process used to make and test theories (predictions) of the world. We test our theories through practice attempts in an effort to develop adaptive patterns (skills) that give us power to survive and thrive. We have brains so that we can create adaptable flexible movement in order to act successfully in the world. Nature gives us examples of how the brain is used to decide movement.

Take, for example, a simple marine animal, the sea squirt. The squirt is born with a brain and nervous system used to swim. When the squirt reaches the juvenile stage, it fixes itself to a rock, where it will stay for the remainder of its life cycle. Once it no longer needs to swim, it digests its brain and nervous system and collects food while stationary (Wolpert, Diedrichsen, and Flanagan, 2011).

The brain creates movement through a process referred to as Bayesian decision theory, which is interesting as well as important for understanding how we make decisions. Researchers studied the brain's processes by observing the hand and eye motions of two children, a child of normal abilities and a child diagnosed with autism, as they played a game of computer Pong. In the game of Pong, hand-eye coordination is required to track and hit a digital ball moving across the computer screen.

Simulators, used in the experiment, revealed that the eyes of the child with autism only followed the ball. His attempts to hit the computer image had low success. However, the other child's eye movements tracked and predicted the movement of the ball, looking in front of where the ball was traveling. When the child successfully predicted the probability of the location of the ball, he was able to hit the ball (Sinha, 2010, 16:02).

ALGORITHMS FOR ACTION

Another example of how the brain works to predict, test, and decide which movements to make is taken from birds. Strogatz (2004), a mathematician, studied flocks of over a million starlings that gathered in England every year. The birds created amazing patterns as they flew through the sky in synchrony. Strogatz took videos of the birds and asked researchers to develop a computer program to simulate the birds' flight patterns.

The computer programmers generated dots on a computer screen to represent the birds and tested many different possibilities using algorithms, or mathematical rules, to direct the movement of the dots in an attempt to recreate the movements of the birds. After many failed guesses, the programmers succeeded using only three rules, or algorithms. Each computer-generated dot was directed to

- move at the same speed;
- use the seven closest dots as reference points and coordinate its movements with them;
- avoid threats.

Threats were defined by the programmers as out-group dots or predators. With these three rules, the computer program simulated a close approximation of the starlings' flight pattern. Interestingly, humans organize in similar ways through the subconscious development of social algorithms called norms.

The Internet is an example of a social algorithm that relies on a very simple set of rules to move a vast array of data across the globe, similar to the synchronous flight of birds. The previous examples reveal how the mind uses the brain to process data to predict the world in order to successfully act and control it. Movement becomes a matter of decision making based on statistical probabilities, for which the normal brain is well suited (Zittrain, 2009).

The ability to make accurate predictions, and practice skills repeatedly over time, is the critical element in developing brain growth and neural networks for flexible skills, creativity, and mastery (Novak and Gowin, 1984). Consider whether you make up stories to explain your behaviors rather than truly self-reflecting to identify the algorithms that may be driving your behaviors.

What are the algorithms for your behavior? What beliefs, or mindsets, do you use for predicting, testing, and guiding your decisions, judgments, and actions? What significance is there in understanding your own algorithms? Could you possibly improve your functioning by creating algorithms for your behavior that are in sync with other individuals with growth mindsets?

MINDSET FOR PREDICTION AND CONTROL

Viewed in this way, our mindset reflects our belief in our abilities to gain skills to predict and control our world. The beliefs are drawn from making predictions and testing the likelihood that our efforts will bring about the outcome we want. If the results are "no," we develop a fixed mindset; a "yes" results in a growth mindset. The mindset predictions we make are used in choosing our goals and the strategies we use to reach them.

A person using a growth mindset believes one's brain can grow and learn. The information in this chapter shows that this belief can be taken quite literally. As you practice developing skills repeatedly over time in a positive constructive environment, you develop new mental maps and new brain cells. This increases your flexibility in new situations, called resilience. Individuals using a growth mindset belief demonstrate greater resilience.

Key points to remember

- Our brain builds progressively from childhood through adulthood creating mental maps of our experiences and the meanings we give to them.
- Memory is state dependent (emotional learning) and can become inaccessible when a person is in a different mental state.
- We have brains so that we can create adaptable flexible movement in order to act successfully in the world.
- Brains actually do grow new cells when we learn, so a growth mindset can be taken literally.

Chapter 5

The Biology of Flexibility

> The measure of a person's strength is not his muscular power or strength,
> but it is his flexibility and adaptability.
>
> —Debasish Mridha

One's flexibility is largely influenced by the accuracy of one's mental maps and ability to adapt to changes in circumstances. Sternberg (1985a) provided a framework for studying the concept of human intelligence that explores the relationship of the individual with one's internal world, external world, and one's experiences. Bandura (2002) developed a similar model, describing influences on learning from, internal thoughts and feelings, external social context, and one's actions/decisions.

A growth mindset is a critically important part of the decision-making and sense-making process used for the development of flexible skills. Following is a discussion of the brain, including a description of various regions and influences involved in a complex interaction necessary for developing meaningful and transformative learning.

Pay attention to the processes related to each region, because an understanding of these different areas and their functions, will help as you read the rest of the book, to understand how having a growth mindset can help you improve and grow. For example, you will read about how the imagination, social context, consciousness, and transcendent values interact and are all necessary elements for developing a growth mindset and achieving your goals.

The brain is only two percent of the body's total weight, yet its activity uses from twenty to twenty-five percent of the body's energy and oxygen. For this discussion, the brain is divided into: two main hemispheres, left and right; a lower brain (including the midbrain); and the prefrontal cortex; each performing a unique function. Figure 5.1 provides a model of the regions of

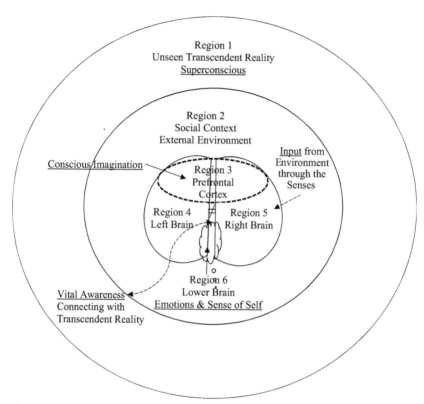

Figure 5.1.   Model of regions of the brain and inputs influencing development.

the brain and their various influences on one's ability to learn and to develop healthy social connections.

REGIONS OF THE BRAIN

Spend some time reviewing the schematic model of the brain provided in the figure in this chapter. Six regions are drawn, though the actual brain is much more complex than this. This simple model of the brain will be used to create a framework for understanding how researchers have described the brain's processes. The brain's functions will be discussed in light of learning processes and mindset beliefs.

Left Hemisphere

The *left hemisphere* (Region 4) processes symbols, thinks in past and future, focuses on details, creates labels and categories, and recalls and communicates memories through language. These past, future, and symbolic functions allow the left brain to think in sequence, often referred to as linear thinking. The conscious part of thinking uses the tools of language so we can communicate with each other and subvocalize to ourselves; the voice you hear in your head when you read silently. (Note: In some individuals the location of the functions may vary).

The Umwelt

The *umwelt* is a scientific term used for the region of conscious sense awareness. The umwelt differs among animals and humans. For example, bats sense objects through air compression waves, and migratory birds sense the earth's magnetic field for finding direction. The human consciousness does not sense these unseen influences.

In fact the normal human brain senses less than one 10-trillionth of what is known to be surrounding us. Neither does the conscious mind sense much of the electromagnetic and mechanical wave spectrum. Visually the brain cannot sense objects much smaller than the width of a human hair (Eagleman, 2015).

Dr. Peter Goram, a physicist, has researched a part of the unseen world as he studied the neutrino. Goram described the neutrino as a force that surrounds us, a force in which we live, yet is a conundrum for scientists. The neutrino was described as determining the kinetics of the production of the elements and was present and involved in the beginning of the physical universe. However, the neutrino seems to exist in a separate dimension.

Goram explained:

> As a physicist, even though I understand [the neutrino] mathematically and I understand it intellectually, it still hits me in the gut that there is something here surrounding me almost like some spirit or God that I can't touch . . . but I can measure it . . . It's like measuring the spirit world. (Herzog, 2007)

Right Hemisphere

The *right hemisphere* (Region 5) can be compared with the parallel processor of a computer, where multiple functions occur simultaneously. The right hemisphere processes emotions and information from the senses, looks for the big picture, takes in elements of context, and creates relationships that are not bounded by time or categories. The flexibility of these associations created in the right hemisphere gives humans a creative capacity.

Sensory Processing Biases

The data coming to our senses is actually different from what our mind brings to our consciousness. An example is our ability to see three dimensions. The eye actually "sees" only two dimensions. The sense of touch and movement provides information to create a third dimension. We correct and adapt our behaviors through experience and memory just as in the game of Pong, previously described. Thus, we develop a sense of dimension in our vision thereby increasing our success at grasping or hitting objects.

Cultural Bias

The *culture in which we are raised* creates a *bias* in the way we think, preferring either a left or right hemisphere orientation. The right and left brain are not equal and do not fully share the maps we create in them to explain our experiences. Our processing preferences are developed partly through the language used by our culture of origin and partly through the social rewards and punishments we receive for our actions. Westerners tend to have a left hemisphere bias.

Prefrontal Cortex

The *prefrontal cortex* (Region 3) is a relatively large part of the brain, located at the front of the left and right hemispheres, and has the capacity to simulate experience, referred to as our imagination. The stories we create are rehearsed in the prefrontal cortex and can synthesize feelings of happiness through our imagination, even when we can't feel real happiness because we don't get what we want (Gilbert, 2006).

In some ways the prefrontal cortex acts like a psychological immune system and emotion regulator, as well as being the seat of moral judgment and rational decision making. This area isn't fully matured until adulthood, requiring education to develop moral standards as a foundation for ethical character development. As Aristotle explained, "The aim of education is to make the pupil like and dislike what he ought" (Lewis, 2002, p. 700).

The Lower Brain

The *lower brain* (Region 6) includes the spinal cord, which enters the base of the brain at the center (midbrain) of the hemispheres. The pons is at the top of the spinal cord and is described as having the unique function of creating mental representations of the *self*. French philosopher Rene Descartes described the mind as consciousness and the body as the sense of self. One's perceptions of limits to the human body develops a sense of "I."

Descartes philosophized that the act of doubting, as reflective thinking, provided logical evidence for the existence of a self (consciousness) apart from the physical self (Descartes and Voss, 1989). Theory of mind has been used as a framework to explore the unseen processes of cognition. However, we must remember that the parts of the individual are integrally connected, not separate, and function as a unity. More will be said about this in a later section.

Senge (1990) explained,

> People are agents, able to act upon the structures and systems of which they are a part. All the disciplines are, in this way, "concerned with a shift of mind from seeing parts to seeing wholes, from seeing people as helpless reactors to seeing them as active participants in shaping their reality, from reacting to the present to creating the future." (p. 69)

The Pineal Gland and Sense of Self

The *pineal gland* (also located in Region 6) has been hypothesized as participating in a connection between the unseen world and the mind. Descartes (1633, 1999 and 1988) suggested the pineal gland connects the brain to the spirit. In figure 5.1, Region 1 represents transcendent reality, or the unseen forces, influencing one's thoughts, aiding in the control of one's visceral self (emotions and drives), and contributing to the ability to act in a social context.

One's capacity to transcend the self-centeredness of the "I," or physical body's limitations, enables a person to develop

- altruistic behavior toward others;
- an awareness of the cause and effect from one's actions;
- a sense of self in relationship to others, without which one remains self-centered;
- and maintain a personal sense of responsibility for and control over one's actions.

The mind contributes to the development of multiple representations of one's sense of self over the life cycle of the individual. Each representation creates physical changes in the brain, as well as different chemical encoding. As infants, the representations of self are first undifferentiated from one's experience of sensations in the body. A sense of a contracted self develops as one becomes aware of the inner and outer boundaries of the body.

This self-centered awareness shifts as the individual matures and creates new pathways and representations through healthy personal and social experiences. Transcendent awareness may also be referred to as *vital awareness* because the individual becomes conscious of the consequences of one's actions and develops one's sense of moral responsibility and accountability.

With transcendent awareness, the "I" moves from being the sole center of consciousness to incorporating representations of others within the self-concept, an expanded sense of self as connected to mankind, and incorporates transcendent referents. The transcendent region compares with a sense of spirituality as Shermer (2007) explained:

> Spirituality is a way of being in the world, a sense of one's place in the cosmos, a relationship to that which extends beyond oneself. . . . Science and spirituality are complementary, not conflicting; additive, not detractive. (pp. 158–159)

The Amygdala

The *amygdala* (in Region 6) is a part of the brain considered to be responsible for emotions and survival drives. Think of this area as controlling the *grasping and getting* drives. When you feel driven to get something, or to reach for something, think of this as coming from a physical (visceral) part of yourself. Many of us battle with ourselves because we haven't controlled the drives from this part of the brain. Transformative learning gives us control over the "visceral self" (Lewis, 2002, p. 703).

CONSCIOUS AND SUBCONSCIOUS PROCESSING

The separate processes of the brain hemispheres have been described as thinking fast (automatically, intuitively, or subconsciously) and slow (conscious focus, judgment, analytic, and the belief that one has the power of personal choice) (Kahneman, 2011). Conscious and subconscious processes of the brain are separate but connected. Too much interconnectivity between the unconscious and conscious can reduce one's mental stability.

The conscious part of the brain can become overwhelmed with too much data (called cognitive load). Therefore, the subconscious memory is not fully accessible to the conscious part, which would be overwhelmed. Pain can be understood, in this regard, as the excess of input without sufficient resources to manage the incoming stimulus.

Our conscious mind protects us from inappropriate influences by deciding what to believe and by identifying what is safe and ethical. The conscious mind acts as a filter, developed during childhood, to identify and label which experiences are good, safe, and connected with one's in-group. One's sense of limits and self-regulation is also supported by this process.

One's memory is used for deciding one's actions. *Our ability to determine our own goals and act collectively to achieve them relies on the management of our learning, or the careful selection of the data we receive and the judgments we assign to it.* Recall that we create meaning and store our memories as patterns for use in responding in future situations.

The brain receives all incoming data as electrical signals, and the mind, using judgments from the conscious filter, attributes meaning and value to the input and stores the information as mental maps on the brain. The conscious brain uses a selective focus, identifying and excluding unsafe sources, unimportant and sometimes important facts, when creating meaning and memory. These processes have survival benefits and are subjective, that is, relate to one's unique needs.

Take, for example, students in school or employees in a corporation. If they perceive their environment as unsafe, the brain has a filter that will block learning in that context. Developing perceptions of justice, equity, and fairness promotes improvements in individual choice to engage new learning. In this book, references to justice, equity, and fairness refer to processes supporting healthy psychosocial factors and use of transcendent values.

When individuals are able to manage their mindset and maximize their power of personal choice, self-organizing actions follow to produce equity, justice, and fairness in other areas.

Practices Influencing the Brain's Processes

Using a *growth mindset* belief helps one to imagine and predict *the future* with a perception of power of personal choice; influencing one's belief in the ability to change and growth. In contrast, *mindfulness* practices act to slow down the brain's electrical wavelength, connect the left and right hemispheres, and create increased awareness of *the present*. Individuals with *regressive learning* think about *the past*. They develop a negative sense of self, a belief in their helplessness, and reduction in the ability to integrate new learning. Most people have experienced, or continue to experience, some level of regressive learning.

Caveat: The brain operates on electrical signals of low wave-length. Twenty-first-century electronic technologies, such as television, telephone, cell phones, and newly developed neural interfaces that send and receive electrical messages through the senses, or devices connecting to the body, can overwhelm and bypass the conscious part of the mind and store data, as memory, directly into the subconscious regions of the brain.

These technologies provide tremendous efficiencies and are expedient for reducing workload and in creating and communicating data. Maximizing one's power of personal choice means controlling the data that gets through the door so one can maintain autonomy and respond in integrity with one's values.

MINDSET AND FLEXIBILITY

The key function of the brain is to predict one's environment and control movement of the body to respond. The process of flexible movement contributes to vitality in individuals, in human relationships, and in the operations of organizations. An understanding of how to manage your mindset can contribute to flexible skills to make the best out of the situations in your life.

To be flexible one must understand one's own needs. This includes recognizing healthy behaviors for self and others, developing skills, and acquiring resources to successfully predict the best way to act. We seek to predict and control our world so we can protect ourselves from threats and move ourselves farther along our path toward our chosen goals.

For example, in the school setting, principals and teachers can demonstrate flexibility by working together in the process of shared leadership, collaborative decision making and communicating in a supportive environment. Healthy organizations create just and equitable processes while retaining a healthy balance between individual identities and social roles (Hanson, 2015; Tarter and Hoy, 2004).

How would you characterize flexibility, or vitality, in a person or organization? Cartoon animators, in their efforts to create lifelike animations, have thought this question through thoroughly. Consider the animation sequence of the Pixar Studio's lamp hopping across the screen in the introductory segment of its films. One of the main reasons viewers perceive the lamp as vital, full of life, is that the artists drew the object in flexible motion, coined in animation terms as "squash and stretch" (Thomas and Johnston, 1981, p. 47). "The response of the viewer is an emotional one, because art speaks to the heart" (p. 15).

Young children are highly physically and psychosocially flexible. Life is full of situations that squash and stretch us. We bend under the limits of life and stretch like a butterfly exiting the cocoon when we choose to make positive meaning out of challenges and adversity. As we age, we become less flexible and must work consciously to maintain and develop healthy flexibility and vigor. A review of your own perceptions and emotions will probably reveal that a healthy vitality comes from the ability to be flexible.

Many students who attend private intervention schools are there because they have been given no limits. One young man gave his reason for why he ended up in a corrective educational setting, "My friends and I have everything we want. We bought everything we can buy, tried everything we wanted to try; sex, drugs, alcohol, partying. There is nothing left for us to do. We don't have a reason to live."

If we try to make sense of the world without limits, we realize that we cannot grow. We truly need limits and challenges so we can come to understand who we are and who we can become. Limits challenge us to change, learn new skills, make positive meaning of new situations, and develop our flexibility.

FLEXIBILITY QUIZ

Table 5.1 The Flexibility Quiz gives you an opportunity to discover your level of flexibility.

Directions: Rate the frequency of your behaviors that are listed in the items in table 5.1. The items describe abilities needed to accept limits and make positive meaning out of one's experiences. After filling in the frequency of your behaviors, follow the directions to calculate your score and find your results. Rate your behaviors from Never = 1 to Always = 6.

Table 5.1. Flexibility quiz

Scale ratings	1	2	3	4	5	6
Items	Never	Irregularly	Occasionally	Frequently	Almost always	Always
1. I am able to make positive meaning out of negative experiences						
2. I accept limits as a healthy part of life						
3. I take time to self-reflect						
4. I seek out new information that is reliable and may be contrary to what I think						
5. I identify my biases and recognize both their positive and negative influences on my thinking and behavior						

(Continued)

Table 5.1. (Continued)

Scale ratings	1	2	3	4	5	6
Items	Never	Irregularly	Occasionally	Frequently	Almost always	Always
6. I have overcome regressive learning by seeking help from healthy others						
7. I am able to maintain my own values while respecting differences in others						
8. I am open to listen to others without judgment or fear						

Calculating Your Score

Fill in the item scores on the following appropriate lines, then add the amounts, and divide the total by eight. This will give you the average score for all items:

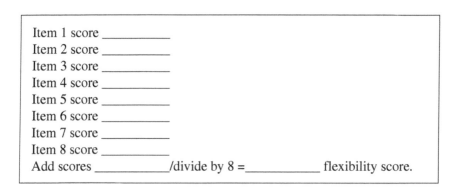

```
Item 1 score _____
Item 2 score _____
Item 3 score _____
Item 4 score _____
Item 5 score _____
Item 6 score _____
Item 7 score _____
Item 8 score _____
Add scores _____/divide by 8 =_____ flexibility score.
```

Understanding the Results

$x \leq 2.0$—Based on how you rated the items on the scale, if your score is two or less, you probably experience life the hard way. You may push against limits in a negative way rather than finding a benefit in your experiences. You may lack respect for others, and especially authority. This would make it difficult for you to find healthy others, who can support you in overcoming regressive learning and internal biases. Read more of this book and make a point of learning more.

Stay open to find the good in yourself and in others around you. Seek healthy others and ask for someone you admire to mentor you on the way to developing a growth mindset. If you need to find physical and emotional safety, you will have to take some chances before you can build trust. Don't give up! You are worth it.

$2.1 \leq x \leq 4.0$—Based on how you rated the items on the scale, you have an average level of flexibility. You may have gotten along in life by having few friends and taking few chances. You are used to the way things are and comfortable with others who are different from you, though being different doesn't automatically mean OK. Sometimes people's differences violate your healthy boundaries, so you are discerning and know how to disconnect to keep safe.

As you read this book, look for ways you can build skills and a broader framework of how to perceive and predict your world. As you build skills, you will find you increase your flexibility score. You may find you can live life more fully.

$4.1 \leq x \leq 6$—Congratulations! Based on how you rated the items on the scale, your level of flexibility is high. A high score on this survey suggests you probably demonstrate resilience, reflexive thinking to overcome biases, and the ability to keep integrity with your deeply held values while respecting others for their differences. Your skills could be useful to mentor others by providing a deeper connection, developing trust, and providing guidance for finding healthy organizations to support skills for a healthier life.

Continue to use the inquiry process to collect quality data, reflect, compare, and reorganize current understanding (Yin, 2014). Develop transformative learning and work with others to align your individual goals with legitimate group goals. You can continue the process for developing growth mindset beliefs in others along the way.

Key points to remember

- Skill development is a cyclical process, requiring many practice attempts, while the brain learns new patterns.
- The highest form of life is the most social and takes the most skills.
- More energy is required in developing new learning as the brain develops cognitive maps.
- Our brain is designed for creating flexible movement to adapt to our world.
- We can use an open inquiry process with others to develop collaborative sense making of the world.

Chapter 6

The "I" and "We" of Identity

Our true reality is in our identity and unity with all life.

—Joseph Campbell

In a world full of noise and competing stimuli, people often experience cognitive overload. The brain seeks to simplify, rather than to work hard, and to use fewer resources. We prefer the simplest solutions and meanings. We feel threatened when our skills are insufficient to respond in new situations, because this reflects poorly on our self-image. We seek experiences that give us positive feelings about how we view ourselves (Ng, Sorensen, and Eby, 2006).

While we seek to protect and affirm our individual sense of self, there is an overarching necessity to develop a healthy social identity. Healthy development includes learning social skills to integrate with those around us in ways that increase our personal power, and the power of those around us, to meet our goals. Sternberg (2005) wrote, "Intelligence [is] the ability to achieve one's goals in life, within one's sociocultural context" (p. 189). As individuals, our success often depends on our ability to get others to help us.

Developing a healthy social identity requires changes in the way one thinks as one matures. A significant role of healthy families, faith organizations, and social organizations is to promote individual development toward a healthy social identity through social contribution.

THE HYDRA AND SOCIAL IDENTITY

The process of developing social identification and contribution can be explored through an analogy of the hydra sea sponge.

Wilson (1907), a biologist studying sea organisms, happened to notice during his experiments that individual cells of a hydra, when separated from the main organism, were able to live independently in the water. He also observed that the individual cells could act independently and crawl around the floor of the container. Intrigued, Wilson performed further studies to determine the nature of the hydra organism.

He mashed a living sea sponge and filtered the pulp through a fine cloth. He obtained masses of individual cells that formed a red cloud in the water of the container. Within eight days, the individual cells had reconstituted into an entire living hydra. Wilson noted that, in the process of reorganizing, these small groups of cells "explored and learned about their environment" (p. 256).

Wilson observed how the individual cells joined together, first in small globules like eggs, and then into groups. Each cell and grouping identified its unique function, or role, in response to others around it. The long-term survival of each cell was extended by its ability to organize with other cells, differentiate its role, and re-create the living form of a new hydra.

SOCIAL ORGANIZATION

Just as the hydra cells were able to identify other hydra cells and join together, individuals can develop social organizations through the process of social identification and role differentiation/social contribution. Social identification occurs through a process of formal and informal communication and support. Acknowledgment from the group generates feelings of belonging. Feelings of trust develop as collective norms (agreed-upon behaviors) develop and are followed by the members (Hanson, Bangert, and Ruff, 2016).

Trust is the belief that others in the group will provide a benefit to us and do us no harm. Glen Pearson (2011), director of the London Food Bank and former Member of Parliament, described a traditional African greeting, *Sawubona,* capturing this idea of individual acknowledgment meaning, "I see your personality. I see your humanity. I see your dignity and respect" (para. 2). The response to *Sawubona* is *Ngikhona,* "I am here" (para. 10).

Pearson explained that the Samburu greeting is a simple method for being present with another and connecting at the heart level. These African greetings demonstrate a collective understanding of common ways of being within the social connection (Bierstedt, 1981). An organization *comes into being* when individuals meet together and form a social contract. Individuals develop a collective identity by developing social norms for behaviors and agreeing to act toward collective goals.

FINDING THE BALANCE BETWEEN "I" AND "WE"

The analogy of the cells organizing into a hydra demonstrates how organizing into groups can contribute to a new social identity. Bandura (2001) wrote, "The essence of humanness is one's personal agency to operate within a context of sociocultural influences" (p. 1). Personal agency means we have a choice on how to act and when to engage. We can withdraw our participation if the group's goals and behaviors are not healthy or are unresponsive to collaborative input.

A healthy organization can be described as social interaction that results in increased individual well-being. The elements of well-being are abstract and so will be described here as comprising three parts:

- the individual's subjective perceptions (happiness);
- one's actual experiences in the social context;
- behaviors that evidence the internal psychological health of the individual (positive functioning). (Page and Vella-Brodrick, 2008, p. 443)

Well-being, one's feeling of happiness, supportive social context, and positive functioning (including psychological and physical health) have been shown to increase when the individuals' goals are aligned with the overall goals of the group. This makes sense because, when goals are aligned, we receive support from others. Individuals combine into groups for the unique and specific purpose of achieving goals. One goal can simply be human connection.

The hydra, in the previous example, is a simple organism with simple goals for survival. Humans, as complex and diverse beings, have diverse needs and goals. As one matures, one learns to strike a healthy balance between one's personal identities and social role(s) and one's personal goals and social contribution. Working together with others toward common goals does not mean that individuals must give all to the group, as in the case of a simple organism.

The ability to act autonomously means understanding when it is appropriate to act independently and when it is appropriate to act within our group role. Our subjective feelings of happiness can become influenced by our desire to have others think well of us and to value our contribution to the group. Sometimes we must shift our priorities from a desire for social approval, and act independently, in order to stay in integrity with our values.

A Blanket against a Cold World

A man, standing in a line one day, began a conversation with the woman next to him. The man said, "It's a cold world. That's what I always say, and there's no blanket." The man's statement highlighted his desire for belonging and support and suggested it wasn't always being met. We can move further along our path toward our goals in each particular social context by recognizing and supporting the needs of others and understanding the signs of healthy organizing.

The ability to accept others requires one to develop a positive self-image and skills to work in a social context. High social skills are necessary to interact in complex social environments and to overcome personal threats to the sense of "I" in the face of personal differences. Working together means responding to others in ways that improve one's functioning and that of others. One is more likely to reach one's goals with healthy social and work relationships.

Does your organization provide a safe place for others, where they sense they are valued for how they see themselves and for who they can be in the group?

Pseudopodia

Even single-celled animals, like the pseudopodia, know how to collaborate in ways that improve their functioning and literally provide a "blanket against the cold world." Sam Bowers, scientist and undersea explorer, observed individual-celled animals, called pseudopodia, which group together to form tree-like shapes in the undersea world of Antarctica (Herzog, 2007). After connecting together, the individual cells drew particles of sand from the sea floor and glued them together to build a protective coating around themselves.

Their collaborative action resulted in a strong collective shape that helped the animals rise above the ocean floor. Once off the floor, the pseudopodia were able to collect food, such as bacteria, from the ocean above. The cooperation between the cells gave them a competitive advantage for survival (Rejcek, 2012, paras 9–14).

A healthy organization embeds behavioral norms that build protective supports for individuals' sense of self-worth, self-efficacy, internal locus of control, and emotional stability (Ng, Sorensen, and Eby, 2006; Wang, Bowling, and Eschleman, 2010). For example, we can recognize and affirm others' strengths and support collective efforts to align personal and group goals. Additionally, we can help others to develop hope and a future time orientation by recognizing the primary needs of individuals in our groups and providing supportive resources.

Not everyone has strong psychosocial protections, but many of the readers of this book probably do have a metaphorical blanket in their families, faith organizations, and social networks. Like the single-celled pseudopodia on the ocean floor, it is important for our survival to ensure we provide psychosocial protections to those with whom we work and live, especially as we are working through problems and challenging ourselves and others to grow.

What does your group do to protect and affirm others, who may live in a cold world without a blanket?

MINDSET AND GOAL ALIGNMENT

Vital leaders, using mindset interventions, understand the importance of aligning the organization's goals and the individuals' goals (Burnette, O'Boyle, Vanepps, Pollack, and Finkel, 2013; Woike, 2008). In a recent study, goal alignment explained 52 percent of the change in a school's growth mindset culture measure. A growth mindset culture contributes to the group's ability to collaborate and plan together leading to collective efficacy (Tarter and Hoy, 2004). Working together with others means to develop common meanings that improve our ability to explain, predict, and control our world.

More important than what one *feels* is what one *believes* about the control one has over one's world. A contributing factor to one's belief about one's power is the level of group support provided to its members to accomplish collective and personal goals. During times of challenge, some individuals continue to achieve their goals while others stop trying. When individuals and groups have growth mindsets, they stay engaged through challenges to reach personal and collective goals.

Goal alignment doesn't mean having the same goals. Goal alignment means ensuring the individual and group goals are *compatible and consistent*. An analogy for goal alignment is the two rails that make up one train track. Two rails, perfectly aligned as one track, support the movement of the train. For example, schools with growth mindset cultures have school-level goals to support all students in their individual goals for growth and learning.

Recall the rules, or algorithms, for how birds can fly in synchrony? We can think of goal alignment, in human social behavior, as following these same algorithms. First, individuals in an organization must move at the same speed, or work together, along the separate individual and group rails of the track. Next, they have to be open to feedback from those around them. Then, the individuals, teams, and system leaders must collaborate to develop rules of behavior and organize to avoid disruptive and negative influences. This includes learning skills to identify how to manage one's behaviors and the hurtful or harmful behavior of others (out-groups or metaphorical predators).

GOAL ALIGNMENT SURVEY

Explore your perceptions about goal alignment in your group or organization by answering the questions in the Goal Alignment Survey in table 6.1.

Table 6.1. Goal alignment survey

Points per item	1	2	3	4	5	6
Items	Strongly disagree	Disagree	Somewhat disagree	Somewhat agree	Agree	Strongly agree
1. The individuals in our group express a full understanding of the group's goals						
2. The goals of the group are aligned with the individuals' needs						
3. Individuals in our group communicate support for the goals of the group						
4. The individuals in the group know how to implement the goals that support the group vision						

Directions: When taking the survey, rate your level of agreement or disagreement with the listed behaviors of your group; examples of groups might be your school, workplace, social group, family, athletic team, or classroom. (Caution: Do not think about your leader's behaviors for this survey. The leader's behaviors are measured on a different survey, not provided here, for collective efficacy).

Rate your level of agreement from Strongly disagree = 1 to Strongly agree = 6).

Calculating Your Score

After filling in your level of agreement or disagreement with the items in the survey, you can calculate your average score using the formula provided.

Item 1 score _____
Item 2 score _____
Item 3 score _____
Item 4 score _____
Add scores _____/divide by 4 =_____ Goal alignment score.

Individual score. After you complete the survey, you can compare your score with others in your group to determine how *each of you* perceive how well your group or organization's goals are aligned with the individuals' goals. Remember when comparing individual results the scores may vary significantly. Your score applies only to *your* perceptions about the group.

Group score. To find your group score, add all the individuals' scores (as calculated earlier) and divide by the number of surveys completed. Then, compare the average you calculated for all survey scores to the mean found in the research ($x = 4.1$). Read a discussion of the following possible results.

Understanding the Results

x ≤ 3.0 is low. If you find your scores are low, based on the answers you or your group provided, your group has room to grow in developing collaborative goals. Don't be discouraged. Collecting data is a beginning to a process of change. Share the results with your group to begin a dialogue about your group's perceptions. Use the strategies described in this book to develop a deeper understanding of how to help your group grow and learn together. Invite others to work together in developing common goals for healthy organizing.

3.1 ≤ x ≤ 4.5 is an average score. Your group's score suggests an ability to recognize individuals' goals in the context of work and collaborate together on routine and team-level activities. Based upon your perceptions, your group contributes to smooth operations though may not necessarily be able to go above and beyond to ensure the best welfare of the organization. Remember to identify individual's strengths and acknowledge their self-perceptions and align their strengths with job roles. Share this book with your group and discuss which ideas you might want to implement.

4.6 ≤ x ≤ 6 is high. Congratulations, based upon self-reports by you and/or your group, the results reveal a high score for aligned goals. The individuals in your group will experience well-being from clearly aligned goals. The individuals feel their jobs promote their personal advancement and growth as well as those of the group. When the group's goals are aligned with individuals' goals, a growth mindset culture can develop.

The group can adapt and grow where there is a strong belief in the ability of the group to work together, solve problems, and create innovations. Vital leadership recognizes and supports the individuals and ensures just processes and provides supports to solve problems in the group. When there is just leadership providing formal structures for collaboration (time for individuals to work together and share leadership), positive social relationships between members can develop.

With positive social relationships, most individuals will go above and beyond their job descriptions to help others and participate in group activities outside the normal time together. This citizenship behavior is a critical element for successful functioning of any organization (Niqab, et al, in process).

Next Steps–Developing Goal Alignment

The following steps are a beginning to the process of developing aligned goals leading to a growth mindset culture in your group or organization.

1. Create time in the day to work and plan together.
2. Read research about developing collective goals and collective efficacy.
   a. Collect information (interviews/focus groups and observations) about the individual's goals, beliefs, and actual behaviors in your group. (Be mindful of how your actions align with your beliefs.)
   b. Compare what is actually being done in your group (theories in action) versus the group's survey results (espoused theories) (Ruff, 2002)
3. Engage in challenging dialogue with your group members using the results of your inquiry.
   a. Compare the survey results with what you find from data collection.
   b. Reflect on individual and group values and how they influence the choice of goals.
4. Discuss ways to align the group goals and the individuals' goals and beliefs so both work together like two rails of one track.
   a. Review the group and individual goals to ensure the goals are contextualized and legitimate.
   b. Respect personal privacy and use discernment.
5. Reorganize, as needed, to develop systems and structures that promote perceptions of justice in individuals in the group.
6. Promote organizational and transformative learning. (Hanson, 2015)

Key points to remember

- While we seek to protect and affirm our individual sense of self, there is an overarching necessity to develop a healthy social identity.
- When we come together in groups to work together toward common goals, we give our permission to act as a collective.
- We give up some independence and begin to develop new ideas of ourselves in our social setting.
- The well-being of the individual depends on the alignment of the individual and group goals.
- We can build trust that leads to an openness to work together when we help others reach their goals and we are careful to do no harm.

Chapter 7

Predicting What Will Make You Happy

Knowing what we want means . . . being able to anticipate accurately how one choice or another will make us feel, and that is no simple task.

—Barry Schwartz, *The Paradox of Choice: Why More Is Less*

Most people want to be happy and are incredibly resilient at finding things to think about that bring them feelings of happiness. Happiness can be described as "a positive state of mind that involves the whole life experience" in combination with "positive functioning" (Page and Vella-Brodrick, 2008, p. 442). How we think influences our happiness, which in turn, influences one's success on the job, in school, and in one's relationships (Achor, 2012, 7:42).

One's feelings can be manipulated by thought processes and by priming from the environment. For example, consider the concept of "retail therapy.' When one feels sad, one may go to the store, or online, and buy some "fast fashion" and, temporarily, *feel* "happier." However, the conditions of our external world contribute only about 10 percent to our overall happiness.

The remaining 90 percent of our happiness depends on how we process our experiences in the world including the connections we make with others (Cloud, 2011). Recall, from the introductory paragraph, true happiness is a combination of thoughts and the nature and quality of one's actual experiences, and is evidenced by one's functional behaviors. Predictors of happiness include being optimistic, developing a strong social network, and viewing stressors as positive challenges, rather than as threats.

Changing the lens through which you view the world, not only changes your perceptions of your happiness, your new mindset can drastically improve your behaviors and your chance of reaching your goals. Seeking happiness is actually more than just a preference for feeling good. Seventy-five percent of one's job success is explained by the same variables that contribute to one's feelings of happiness including; beliefs, social support, and how one handles stress.

HAPPINESS AND SOCIAL CONNECTION

The number one predictor of happiness is frequent positive involvement in committed social relationships. "[T]he only thing that really matters in life [is] your relationships to other people" (Shenk, 2009, approximately para. 52). Positive social interactions help individuals develop priorities that can be used to choose constructive goals. People of all ages need positive mentoring to appreciate the importance of a future orientation and to develop discipline for power to delay gratification and to maintain focus on the goals.

Growth Mindset and Connection

The most common method people use to accomplish the goal of feeling good is to try to control and predict what will happen to them (Dweck and Leggett, 1988; Novak, 2002; Senge, 2009). However, predicting and controlling our world can be difficult, because we live and work with people, whose goals may not align with ours. Developing shared goals allows us to internalize meaningful goals of others as well as receive help from others. A growth mindset belief (that we can grow our brains and learn through our own effort) is part of the formula for happiness and is a result of the cycle of happiness.

The ability to create positive meaning from life's experiences creates a "happiness advantage" that leads to increased social engagement, willingness to put in effort to achieve goals, and improved results. It is the cumulative effect of repeated positive face-to-face experiences that creates deep connection (Achor, 2012, 10:03). For example, research suggests that attending a religious service provides only a small benefit. However, attending religious services routinely over time provides a huge benefit.

Habits of Happiness

It is important to practice habits that feed positive thoughts and feelings into the cycle of goal attainment leading to well-being. Recall how one's mindset produces a narrowing of focus on a priority goal? Managing where your mind goes, focusing rather than wandering, is the first step because this will direct your body's actions. You can begin to manage your mindset to increase your power of personal choice.

The first item on the following list of *habits of happiness* is taking time to self-reflect. Self-reflection is a recursive process that supports insight into one's thoughts, feelings, and actions; that is, the individual consciously reframes prior experiential learning and creates new productive meaning (Rossi and Cheek, 1988, p. 162).

We also increase our potential for success and feelings of happiness as we see others benefit from our joint efforts. Social interactions are much more complex than individual behaviors. This list will help identify steps you can take to promote feelings of happiness that lead to positive social experiences and improved engagement and well-being:

- Reflect (meditate)
- Exercise
- Sufficient sleep
- Acts of altruism (volunteerism)
- Communicate gratitude ("The Science Behind the Smile," 2012, p. 6).

THE CYCLE OF HAPPINESS

The cycle of happiness is not linear. Happiness can be seen as an output along the cycle as well as an input. Social connection can provide supports that would be out of the individual's control. Developing positive social networks helps you to identify productive goals, learn from others how to manage your emotions, learn discipline to focus your mind on the tasks, and overcome obstacles.

Figure 7.1 shows a model of variables leading to happiness and a growth mindset culture.

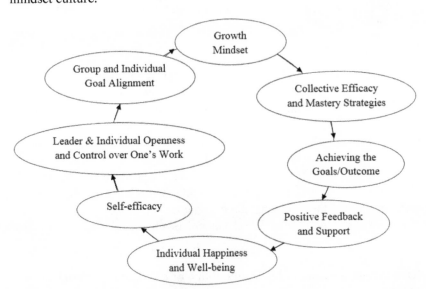

Figure 7.1. Model of variables leading to successful goal attainment and feelings of happiness.

A brief review of these variables and others contributing to goal attainment in the cycle of happiness follows.

Openness to Change and Intrinsic Work Locus of Control

The concept of personal agency, or control over one's environment (intrinsic work locus of control), is central to the model of mindset (Spector, 1988).

Example of Openness to Change

An example of how one can reach one's goals by being open to change is provided here. A successful young administrator shared some of his personal background. For purposes of sharing his story, he will be called Alex. Alex explained that he didn't have a father available to be his role model when he was a child. Alex didn't feel resentful or feel sorry for himself. Instead, he observed his friends at school and noticed one's father as being especially helpful and involved.

Alex sought out his friend's father and shared that he admired him and asked him if he would be willing to act as his mentor. The friend's father agreed and the two have met once per month ever since. Alex is now a successful and admired school administrator. He attributed his success to the kindness and support of his friend's father, who acted as his mentor. Alex's success is also the result of his belief in his potential for growth and his openness to change and grow. He reached out to seek help.

Work Locus of Control

Recall in the section on learning how an individual's intrinsic motivation contributed to one's willingness to engage new learning? The same is true at the organizational level. When members work together with the organization's leadership to align goals, the leader must empower them to be heard and act on their input where possible. As individuals see their contributions valued, their sense of power increases.

Research in school growth mindset cultures revealed the administrator's influence had a large impact on the faculty perceptions of the school's growth mindset. The following three variables were shown in a research study to explain approximately 62 percent of changes in school mindset mean scores

- leader support of individuals' autonomy, or one's sense of control over one's work,

- leader's openness to change
- followers' openness to change was influenced by the leader's openness and belief in growth. (Hanson, Ruff, and Bangert, 2016)

Caveat: Being open to change doesn't mean that all change is worthwhile. Administrators and leaders must be given reliable evidence that any change that is not initiated collaboratively, would provide a benefit to those they lead, before they would be open to lead others in the change (Aslan, Beycioglu, and Konan, 2008).

"An open mind, in questions that are not ultimate, is useful. But an open mind about the ultimate foundations either of Theoretical or of Practical Reason is idiocy," and "you will destroy all values, and so destroy the bases of your own criticism" (Lewis, 2002, p. 716).

Goal Alignment

"In life, as in football, you won't go far unless you know where the goalposts are" ("Facts about Arnold," n.d., para. 17). A variety of influences impact the progress one makes along the path to happiness and well-being. Some of these variables are malleable, or can be changed through effort, and others are outside of one's individual control. Control over these variables increases when individuals in an organization have developed the ability to work well together.

Goal alignment, discussed in the previous chapter, is an integral part of the cycle of happiness. Goal alignment is the result of conscious efforts of the organizational leadership to work together with members as a whole and develop shared goals. The goals must be explicit and a plan developed to get there (Blackwell, 2012). In order for the process of goal alignment to take place, both the leaders and members must be open to collaborate and share power. When leaders share power, they enable the members to increase their decision making along with their intrinsic work locus of control (Hanson, 2015).

Growth Mindset

Organizational-level growth mindset refers to a shared belief in the collective ability of an organization to help individuals learn and grow. Just as an organization's mindset culture can develop self-organizing processes that lead to health and vitality, so an individual's mindset influences one's self-organizing and self-monitoring behaviors. Both the individual's and organization's mindset influences the type of goals that they will choose.

Individuals and organizations with growth mindset beliefs have been shown more often to choose mastery goals that challenge the individual to learn and grow. Individuals with fixed mindsets tend to choose performance goals, ones where they can feel successful and receive positive feedback for performance, such as earning grades (Delaney, Dweck, Murphy, Chatman, and Kray, 2015). The next sections provide a discussion of these two types of strategies.

Strategies to Reach the Goal

Mastery Strategies

People with growth mindsets have been shown to routinely put energy into mastering the skills necessary to achieve their goals. Teachers and workplace managers can support mastery learning in their students, or employees, by allowing more time to practice new skills in context; providing specific, positive, step-by-step feedback in a just-in-time fashion, from someone the learner trusts; and teaching psychosocial skills for self-regulation and persisting through challenges.

A school's use of mastery strategies was shown to correlate highly with a school's growth mindset culture. Mastery strategies include

- support for mistakes as part of the learning process;
- an emphasis on effort over achievement;
- framing learning as fun;
- focusing on understanding over memorization;
- providing relevant tasks (Midgley et al., 2000).

Performance Strategies

Teachers and workplace managers with a performance emphasis (also called academic press) provide their followers with challenging work, hold them to high standards, and press them to achieve. A performance (academic) emphasis correlated with the leader's self-efficacy beliefs, not with the use of mastery strategies. This is an important distinction to recognize for administrators, teachers, and parents.

An *academic (performance) emphasis* puts the focus on outcomes. Grades can be seen as payment for achievement. When schools, teachers, students, and parents view good grades as the goal, rather than as a means to mark progress toward realistic goals that are intrinsic to the learner, this can create perceptions of injustice in students and result in withdrawal behaviors (Herrmann and Brandstätter, 2015).

All students have unique situations and various levels of support at home. Students who come to the classroom less advantaged (lacking background in the course content, sufficient food, shelter, basic health care, or positive emotional supports) may not be able to master the content in the set amount of time. Actual and perceived inequities in the design of educational systems can reduce trust in students and create fixed mindset beliefs.

When individuals of any age fail to receive sufficient financial, physical, and psychosocial supports, they can't meet realistic goals for themselves, their well-being and happiness go down. Insufficient resources can cause a lack of future orientation, loss of hope, poor decision-making, hedonistic behavior, sense of helplessness, and reduced functioning (Bregman, 2017).

No one can achieve completely independently. We all need a "blanket in a cold world" to develop autonomy and manage our mindset so we have power to maximize our power of personal choice to learn and grow.

Collective Efficacy

Collective efficacy develops from an openness to change the existing patterns of relationships and behaviors and to behave in alignment with values that protect the welfare of others. Social norms can be embedded in the formal structure of the system.

Collective efficacy is a "people's shared belief in the collective power of the group to produce desired results" (Bandura, 2001, p. 14). Collective efficacy is the temperature of a healthy organization (Tarter and Hoy, 2004). The groups' willingness to set higher goals, persist in the face of setbacks, have high motivation, and achieve greater levels of accomplishments increases with its collective efficacy.

Individual and group efficacy beliefs are key components in the literature on organizational learning theories. A growth mindset culture contributes to the collective efficacy of the organization. Collective efficacy and mastery strategies have been shown to directly explain improvements in organizational outcomes in schools (Blackwell, 2012; Hanson, 2015; Hoy, Tarter, and Kottkamp, 1991; Murphy and Dweck, 2010; Tarter and Hoy, 2004).

Bandura (2001) warned that our social future is being changed by the erosion of collective efficacy caused by rapid technological advancements, changing the way individuals and nations relate to their world. We can make a better future, and world, by understanding the influences system structures have on our social experiences (p. 23).

Feedback

A variety of variables contribute to an individual's decision to engage goals and persist through challenges. When learners receive constructive feedback in the form of support to develop psychosocial skills in context, they exhibit higher attendance, work and study habits, and actively organize learning materials (Farrington et al., 2012). The following perceptions of the feedback one receives contribute to one's decision to persist toward a goal or withdraw:

- Is there a threat to the ego (–) or a feeling of well-being (+)?
- Is task-specific information provided to make corrections (+) or no step-by-step instructions provided (–)?
- Does the rate of progress toward the goal seem sufficient for the effort?
- Is there a sense of trust (developed by perceptions of the reliability of the source, voice tone, and body language)?
- Are there sufficient resources and power (+) to achieve the goal?
- Is there a future time orientation that provides power to delay gratification (+) or is there a feeling of helplessness (–)?

If the feedback is perceived as sufficient and constructive, then the receiver will

- develop a willingness to choose more challenging goals;
- challenge one's current understandings;
- persist through challenges because he or she will delay gratification for future gain;
- be open to correct errors in prior assumptions;
- perform repeated practices over time and develop transferable learning (mastery learning) (Hong, Chiu, Dweck, Lin, and Wan, 1999).

Well-Being

Individual well-being is considered present when the individual demonstrates the ability to accept himself or herself, self-regulates emotions, has an accurate perception of reality, can act with autonomy toward achieving his or her implicit goals, shows mastery over his or her environment, grows, develops, and has an integrated personality (Hong, Chiu, Dweck, and Sacks, 1997).

Organizations are much like individuals. Their social norms develop and grow and have life cycles. In open systems a healthy organization is flexible and can adapt because individuals have high autonomy and the system rules and regulations are less rigid. The leadership distributes power and aligns the organizational goals with the individuals in them. Recall that to be an organization two things are required, recognition of each other (social identity) and an agreement to work together toward shared goals.

As a healthy organization grows and matures, its agents take proactive steps to ensure moral imperatives are recognized and incorporated into the actions of the group. These actions become memories of the individuals about how to act in the group; new meaning is made. Importantly, a healthy organization will develop socially just processes, procedures, and equitable distribution of resources.

The healthy organization ensures against individual agendas and isolated voices that attempt to dominate and control the collective dialogue, agenda, and group's resources.

The following are indicators of organizational well-being. The system

- fosters hope and resilience in its individuals;
- shows vitality at the organizational level;
- is able to retain employees long-term;
- aligns organizational goals with the individuals' goals;
- aligns skills and strengths with job tasks;
- has a greater than 7:1 ratio of good experiences to bad;
- enables employees to turn beliefs into action;
- has greater than 5:1 positive to negative speech acts between employees (Page and Vella-Brodrick, 2008).

HAPPINESS FROM GOAL PURSUIT SURVEY

Take the Happiness from Goals Pursuit Survey in table 7.1, designed to help you discover what motivates your choice of goals. You may be surprised at what you learn. The group's average results from this survey provide data to begin the challenging dialogue about the perceived preferences of the group toward specific behaviors as valued and supported.

Directions: Arrange the following items from 1 = Highest contribution to good feelings to 12 = Lowest contribution to good feelings by writing the numbers from 1 to 12 next to the items in the list. Then follow the instructions to learn how to calculate your results. (Children under twelve years of age, may use only the first six items on the scale.)

Table 7.1. Happiness from Goal Pursuit Survey

When I feel good after a certain event it is because:

Item	Rank order (1–12)
1. I helped someone else	_____
2. I did my best	_____
3. Someone else helped me to be successful	_____
4. I did what someone else wanted	_____
5. I worked hard together with others to achieve the goal	_____
6. I got closer to my personal best	_____
7. I focused on the goal	_____
8. I received personal recognition for my accomplishment	_____
9. I am responsible and met my responsibility	_____
10. My personal interests are aligned with the group activity	_____
11. I got what I wanted	_____
12. I received personal recognition for my effort	_____

Calculating Your Score

Next, copy each of your ratings, the numbers from 1 to 12 that you wrote on your completed survey above, to the items on table 7.2. Notice which *Motivation* letter *(E, I, or SC)* is most often associated with your four top choices (ratings 1, 2, 3, and 4). Read the descriptions that follow to understand your results.

E = extrinsic, (motivated by what others say or think); I = intrinsic, (motivated by personal interests); and SC = social contribution, (motivated by providing a benefit to others).

Table 7.2 Scoring rubric for Happiness from Goal Pursuit Survey

Table 7.2. Scoring rubric for Happiness from Goal Pursuit Survey

When I feel good after a certain event it is because:

Item	Rank order (1–12)	Motivation (S, I, E)
1. I helped someone else	_____	SC
2. I did my best	_____	I
3. Someone else helped me be successful	_____	E
4. I did what someone else wanted	_____	E

When I feel good after a certain event it is because:		
Item	Rank order (1–12)	Motivation (S, I, E)
5. I worked hard together with others to achieve the goal	_____	SC
6. I got closer to my personal best	_____	I
7. I focused on the goal	_____	I
8. I received personal recognition for my accomplishment	_____	E
9. I am responsible and met my responsibility	_____	SC
10. My personal interests are aligned with the group activity	_____	SC
11. I got what I wanted	_____	I
12. I received personal recognition for my effort	_____	E

Understanding the Results

Individual Scores

Extrinsic (E)—If you rated items with an (E) as highest, then based on your ratings, your good feelings come from what others tell you about yourself. This is called extrinsic motivation. You may be in a competitive environment where you are supported and rewarded for individual excellence and achievement. Extrinsic beliefs come from environments where one has experienced limited personal control. Behaviorist theory suggests individual learning is the result of external rewards and punishments.

Children under twelve will most often have extrinsic (E) motivators; their sense of what defines them is still developing. Children rely heavily on those around them while developing personal identities. A fixed mindset belief often exists with individuals who are extrinsically motivated. They may lack a belief in their ability to grow and learn. They may not have confidence they will receive the help and support they need to reach their goals.

If you are over twelve years old and rated extrinsic motivation as your predominate source of motivation, you may be in an environment that doesn't support personal autonomy or independent action. Some environments are not designed for supporting individual free choice. Sometimes individuals are even punished for seeking personal goal attainment because the group or organization did not seek to align the larger goals with the individuals' goals.

Finding a group, or organization, that has goals that align with your individual values will help you to; find support, develop the ability to feel safe, build trust, and contribute to other's goals, while being able to understand and seek your own growth and interests.

Intrinsic (I)—If you rated mostly intrinsic (I) motivators as your priorities, then based on your ratings, you are motivated by feelings of self-motivated goals. You may prefer to work independently. You probably have the ability to delay getting things you want in order to obtain success in the future.

Intrinsic motivation develops from a sense of personal power and control (growth mindset) and support from others with resources to help you achieve your personal goals. Doing what you love just feels good and you can put effort into getting the things you want. Intrinsic motivation is highly rewarding in combination with healthy extrinsic motivators such as positive feedback from others for your effort.

Focusing on your goals to the exclusion of supporting others may cost you some relationships and healthy social connections. Be cautious in over focusing on personal goals. Spend time with healthy others, who may not be as driven and single-focused as you. Think of ways you can contribute to others from the heart. One can use self-reflection to develop transformative learning leading to an increasing sense of identification with others.

Social contribution (SC)—If your top ratings were for items of social contribution, you derive happiness from seeing others achieve and from helping the group toward its goals. You may have a tendency to do more than you should at the expense of your own well-being. You may need to be cautious not to be taken advantage of by others.

If a motivator of social contribution develops from positive experiences with others in a setting that promotes equity and social justice, you probably can feel safe that others will contribute equitably to the group. A sense of identity that comes from caring for the group can also be developed as one matures. High *SC* is also associated with collectivist cultures, or a sense of identity with diverse groups.

Mixed—If you found it difficult to rank the items in order from 1 to 12 you may have high flexibility and recognize the influence of the context on what motivates you. You may be able to move along the continuum of a flexible mix of extrinsic, intrinsic, and social contribution, instead of one motivator predominating. As previously described, one usually finds one's current or prior context and culture has shaped one's belief about one's ability to have control over one's world. You may be fortunate to have a supportive and healthy environment that allows you to adapt and be flexible based upon the circumstances.

As individuals grow and develop, extrinsic goals often turn to intrinsic goals, and eventually to social contribution goals. This compares similarly to the idea of Maslow's hierarchy of needs.

Group results–To find the group results, average the individuals' results and identify the motivation that is the most common.

Extrinsic goal (E) —If the group has a high average *(E)* associated with the top rankings, the group probably rewards individual accomplishment and competition.

Intrinsic goals (I) —If the group has a high *(I)* associated with the top rankings, individual autonomy, decentralized management and shared decision making will be supported. The group provides resources to support individuals to perform the tasks.

Social contribution (SC)—If the group value *(SC)* is highest, then the organization (e.g., classroom, team, administration) has probably aligned individual and group goals, leadership demonstrates just practices and equitable decision making, trust is high, and individuals work well together.

Next Steps in the Cycle of Happiness

Next steps—Your task is to reflect on your beliefs, skills, and openness to change and grow. Identify one or two areas where you have influence to challenge yourself, and begin to manage your mindset and learn new skills to maximize your power of personal choice so you can make progress today along the path toward reaching your goals.

In summary, a growth mindset is a belief that one can change through effort and that the change will help one achieve one's goals. A growth mindset requires an intrinsic (internal) sense of control over one's environment (locus of control). Also, the leader's, as well as the followers', openness to learn and to provide support to others contributes to an organization's growth mindset culture and to the development of the individual's beliefs one can reach one's goals within the context of the organization or group.

Key points to remember

- A growth mindset belief (that one can grow one's brains and learn through one's own effort) is part of the formula for happiness.
- People with growth mindsets have been shown to routinely put energy into mastering the skills necessary to achieve their goals.
- How we think, and our happiness, influences our success on the job, in school, and in our relationships.
- Self-reflection is the first step in managing your mindset and maximizing your power of personal choice to focus on positive goals that lead to happiness and well-being.
- An increased sense of well-being and happiness results from a combination of intrinsic locus of control over one's work and one's ability to contribute socially.

Chapter 8

Gross National Happiness

> Always recognize that human individuals are ends, and do not use them as
> means to your end.
>
> —Immanuel Kant

What would happen if we used growth mindset in our daily lives and organized for happiness using social connection and transcendent referents? Developing a growth mindset can be accomplished by considering alternative ways to reflect on and to measure our behaviors. We can also consider different goals as outcomes of the systems in which we work and learn.

For example, one country changed its outcome measure from gross national product (GNP) to gross national happiness (GNH), using the individuals' well-being as the new goal. The following section provides a look into how the country of Bhutan changed its mindset and, resultantly, the measurement methods used for the nation's productivity.

Bhutan is a small country in the Eastern Himalayas of Asia. The Bhutanese leaders took a unique approach to measuring well-being in their country. In 1970, the fourth king of Bhutan first announced the aspiration to be "a country where progress was holistic, inclusive, equitable and sustainable. Where political and spiritual matters were in balance" (Tobgay, 2016, p. 2).

While the GNP has been widely considered the best measure of a country's progress and development, Bhutan developed an outcome measurement indicator called gross national happiness. The GNH includes nine domains; (1) psychological well-being, (2) health, (3) education, (4) time use, (5) cultural diversity and resilience, (6) good governance, (7) community vitality, (8) ecological diversity and resilience, and (9) living standards (p. 6).

A quote from the keynote address by the honorable prime minister of Bhutan, Lyonchoen Tshering Tobgay (2016), to the International Conference on

Gross National Happiness described the rationale for the change, "Indicators are powerful. What we count matters. What we count ultimately influences the policy agendas and decisions of governments" (p. 5). How has the country performed under this new measure?

As the prime minister explained, the significance of the measure is in the *use of what the country values* as a worthy indicator of what to measure. As a result, the government has *shifted its focus* to consider domains not included under the GNP measure. The Bhutanese demonstrated key features of a growth mindset culture. They identified their key values underlying their implicit theories.

The Bhutanese redirected their focus to attend to something new. Using their new focus, they changed how they interpreted and processed the data. A review of the previous chapters in this book may provide insights into how you, the reader, can reflect on your values and shift how you measure your behaviors. One can learn to manage one's mindset and shift one's focus to what is important to growth, health, happiness, and well-being for oneself and others.

OUTCOME MEASURES OR MARKERS FOR GROWTH

Measurement criteria are used for judging policies and practices and reflect underlying values, such as well-being in the case of Bhutan (Guthrie, Garms, and Pierce, 1988). Criteria are necessary to determine if the targeted outcomes of the group, or system, are being met. When using market norms, increased profit is often used as the outcome criteria of success. Efficiency and expedience are often used as the standard by which organizations and systems are judged for their accomplishments. These measures are not necessarily the best indicators of a healthy system.

For example, a system may have a strong bottom line though the feedback loops may be limited. There may be a high division of labor that separates the individuals from the decision-making processes within the system. Former Wall Street analyst Cathy O'Neil described the focus on efficiency under business market norms this way:

> This culture absolutely selects for psychopathic pickers—people who have absolutely no empathy whatsoever, because once you have successfully cleaved off ethical considerations you are incredibly efficient. (Round, 2015)

One's values, as previously explained, can be in conflict with each other depending on the circumstances or context of the situation. An example of conflicting values in context is the use of the atomic bomb during World War II. Officials focusing on reducing long-term casualties expressed that use of the bomb was an expedient means to end the war, potentially saving millions of lives. A conflicting value was expressed by many scientists, who had worked on the bomb's development, stating its use at any time would be inhumane.

Individuals often differ in their priority of beliefs (values) used in decision making. A pragmatic viewpoint was provided by Reverend Marsden (2003), a minister and scholar studying the Māori culture in New Zealand. A Māori leader had heard about the atom bomb used in World War II and questioned Marsden about his experiences in the war. A brief recount of the dialogue follows.

The Māori leader asked, "Do you mean to tell me that the scientists have managed to rend the fabric of the universe?" Marsden answered, "Yes." The leader's response, "But do they know how to sew it back together again?" "No!" (p. 57).

What happens when one's personal values conflict with one's organization or group? You can use a growth mindset to reach out and help lead others to growth. Organizational growth mindset and group level mindset scales are tools used to quantify, or measure, perceptions of a mindset culture. The results can be used to begin a dialogue with the members about their beliefs. Discussions can include ways to reflect collective values in the decision-making process and goals.

NEXT STEP—WISDOM

Gertrude Stein was said to have asked the following question on her death-bed, "What is the answer?" When no one could give her an answer, she then asked, "In that case, what is the question?" (Sternberg, 1985b, p. 1111). Asking the right questions is a necessary precedent to obtaining helpful answers. Wisdom provides us with the ability to ask questions and form answers using a balanced perspective on life while understanding its complex interactions, and the artful use of intuition and judgment (Korac-Kakabadse, Korac-Kakabadse, and Kouzmin, 2001, p. 213).

The Māori people's tradition explains the difference between *knowledge* and *wisdom* this way:

> Now knowledge and wisdom are related but different in nature. Knowledge, [is] a thing of the head, an accumulation of facts. Wisdom is a thing of the heart. It has its own thought processes. It is there that knowledge is integrated for this is the centre of one's being. (Marsden, 2003, p. 59)

Wisdom is associated with the *integration* of previously acquired knowledge. Younger ages are associated with the acquisition of *knowledge* and development of *learning* through life experiences. Maturity is associated with the development of understanding, how the knowledge one acquires through life relates to self, others, the world, and the spiritual (Korac-Kakabadse, Korac-Kakabadse, and Kouzmin, 2001; Marsden, 2003).

Lewis (2002) explained that enlightenment is the result of alignment of one's beliefs with the truth. Self-reflection is necessary to correct errors in knowledge structures and develop transcendent values (beyond self-interest). In review, the use of prior learning, as a source for decisions and actions, is safest when an individual has knowledge stored from the processes of *transformative learning,* a necessary precedent to developing wise judgments.

Metaphor for Finding Wisdom

The Māori tell a story that depicts the transition of young people from childhood to adulthood, becoming capable of contributing to the social fabric of society (Marsden, 2003, p. 59). A paraphrase of the story follows.

A young man sets out in a canoe in the morning to go fishing on the sea. As he paddles out to sea, water sprays up from the bow as it hits the waves. The young man is dampened by the water. The morning sun rises in the sky, sending light through the drops and creating a rainbow in the spray. The spray symbolizes the young man's experiences as he moves through life. Each droplet represents some meaning he has given to his experiences.

The sun rising represents the young man's growing spiritual awareness, and the rainbow symbolizes the integration of his personal meanings, as memories, into a proper transcendent perspective. As the sun rises fully and lightens the spray, the young man now sees all the individual experiences in relationship with the truth (the sun that was hidden behind the horizon). When he understands his relationship to God, man, and the world, his mind is transformed.

The learning that results is what transforms the child into a man who is able to receive the deeper knowledge of the tribal leaders, because he is trusted to use it for good and no longer selfishly. According to Māori tradition, the information and knowledge created in the young man's mind before his enlightenment was understood only through the lens of his self-consciousness.

With transformation, his knowledge is put into a meaningful order, releasing conflicting tensions and contradictions, previously experienced because of a lack of integration. The Māori custom explains further,

> Knowledge is transformed into wisdom. This is essentially a spiritual experience. Illumination is from above, a revelation gift from God. When it occurs, it acts as a catalyst integrating knowledge to produce Wisdom. (Marsden, 2003, p. 59)

Wisdom is a higher knowledge because it transcends self and incorporates the use of truth, justice, and love apart from the corruption of ego, or individual biases, used to protect a positive self-image. To be wise is to be connected with an open heart to truth. Knowing truth becomes the deepest conviction, value, and safeguard for awareness of one's potential for error.

Proverbs 25:2 states, "It is the glory of God to conceal a thing: but the honor of kings is to search out a matter." *Moral conscience* becomes the development of individual cognitive ability to be aware of what actions would bring an increased vitality, or well-being, to self and those around us. Healthy systems and organizations embed transcendent values in the processes and standards for accountability in its members.

Vital leaders in our systems and institutions have authority and obligation to seek out and correct inequities, crime, violence, vice, and corruption. *Maturity* is included in the domain of ethical leaders' values and behaviors reflected by the construct of integrity between one's espoused (or stated) values and values in action, including

- setting clear standards;
- holding others accountable;
- fair distribution of rewards;
- transparency (Yukl, Mahsud, Hassan, and Prussia, 2013).

Ensuring procedural and organizational justice brings order through accountability for individual's behaviors in systems, and between legal entities and societies (Hanson, Loose, Reveles, and Hanshaw, 2017). Transcendent values, such as forgiveness (hiding a matter), can bring healing and restore vitality and trust to previously troubled systems once redirection and correction to safe behavior and processes have been made. An example of a restored organization will be provided in the section on NUMMI.

TRUTH AND LIES

Truth and lies can be considered as opposites of one another. What is lying? The word *lying* has an implicit judgment assumption within its meaning, suggesting a divergence from an absolute reality or, at least, a reality that can be known and agreed upon. Now, recall how we use inaccurate memories as information to judge and attribute causation to our own and others actions. We attempt to predict and control our world through belief, and faith, in the possibilities of the unseen future we imagine for ourselves.

Truth

Truth is an abstract concept that relates to ideas of social norms and ethics. Thomas Paine (1792), one of the founding fathers of the United States, wrote,

"But such is the irresistible nature of truth that all it asks, all it wants, is the liberty of appearing" (para. 2). In this vein, truth is used as the ultimate, or transcendent (supersedes one's self), standard, for guiding and evaluating our actions, thoughts, and beliefs.

If truth needs liberty to appear, then where does this liberty come from? MacIver (1917) explained, "Liberty is the final condition of all progress." He also explained that the word liberty is often misused and "inscribed on the banners of the blindest and most selfish defenders of unjust privilege old or new" (pp. 305 and 306). A discussion of how the misuse of words can result in logic errors and unjust advantages for a few is provided in the chapter titled Language and Communication in this book.

Truth can be viewed as a personal moral referent, residing just beyond the horizon, out of sight, yet available through faith in its existence. For example, a sailor on a ship moves constantly toward the horizon, never reaching it. If the sailor failed to believe in the existence of a destination beyond the horizon, the ship would be lost for want of a direction.

Truth needs an element of faith, or trust, because we do not always see the whole picture. Recall the example of a man running up from behind and grabbing and pushing another man in an alley. Without the broader view of the situation, you would not have sufficient information to determine the truth about the first man's intentions. We all need a measure of faith and vital awareness to recognize there is more to life than seen with the human eye (Vucinic, 2005).

Truth is the representation of unseen existence used as a guide to direct one's actions through a belief in its existence. Truth is preexisting and eternal, collapses time and space, is relevant in all contexts, and embedded in all experiences. Individuals and groups seek to access truth for three purposes:

- As a direction, or path
- As a standard for correction
- As the source of vitality

A growth mindset belief in one's potential to grow and learn means one believes one can become better than before. To improve, one must imagine oneself into the future, or project a future image of improvement, and set a higher goal to move toward. One must become optimistic to see oneself as better than one is viewed in the present.

Overclaiming

This future thinking and prediction becomes a memory that we begin to believe, eventually giving us power to persist through challenges. For example, sports teams project themselves into images of victory even when their prior statistics suggest otherwise. Advertisers are legally allowed to "puff-up" claims about their products. Independent expression supports imagination, creativity, and innovation. Highly creative people have a higher tendency to overclaim their capabilities.

Is this considered lying? Studies of married couples found that the happiest couples, with the most enduring marriages, were those where the partners saw each other as better than they actually were. The partners overclaimed their partner's qualities and created an improved sense of appreciation in each other. Actually, this process of projecting an improved self-image and performance *is necessary* for growth and is part if the process of a growth mindset.

Lies

Lying, on the other hand, is related to issues of ethics and morality, not the use of one's imagination to project a positive future outcome, or remembering overly ambitious perceptions of past outcomes. Lying interferes with productive communication, relationships, resource allocation, and fair and ethical decision making.

If a person intends to harm someone, take something that doesn't belong to them, or knowingly cheat to gain advantage, then communications meant to deceive for personal benefit would be lying. A healthy, developed, moral conscience would intervene and cause one to reflect against communications intended to misrepresent unethical behavior as appropriate. Where there is no moral conscience, the rule of law is a process in social structures designed to promote safety and equity.

The use of internalized transcendent values, developed through reflection and modeling, enables ethical communication and behaviors to support healthy, just, and fair organizations.

The soul then ought to conduct the body, and the spirit of our minds, the soul. This is therefore the first Law, whereby the highest power of the mind requireth obedience at the hands of all the rest. (Hooker in Lewis, 2002, p. 738)

THE POWER OF PERSONAL CHOICE

In review, one increases one's power of personal choice to act in integrity when one focuses appropriately and uses self-reflection. One can seek to uncover and understand one's implicit theories and to internalize transcendent values, leading to vital awareness. One can develop positive social relationships that support healthy perceptions of the self and reality. We can empower ourselves to act in ways that others view us as trustworthy.

Trust is a necessary antecedent to collective efficacy. Recall trust is a belief that others will provide a benefit to us and do us no harm. Trust supports a cohesive integration of activities, cooperation, and perception of stability (Reed, Vidaver-Cohen, and Colwell, 2011). Growing and learning takes effort, repeated practice, and support from others through organizing for collective efficacy.

When one develops or expands one's self-discipline to control personal thoughts, exercise the mind and body, and squash and stretch oneself, new levels of health and well-being result. However, when we are self-centered, we may make up stories to cover up bad behaviors that hurt others. If we use feedback only from ourselves, we are less able to correct these errors.

Have you developed habits of reflection and identified a set of external standards that you can hold as priority beliefs? Are you flexible in your approach to thinking and learning? You can explore new ways to improve your relationships, environment, and support others with whom you work, live, and play.

Key points to remember

- Developing a growth mindset can be accomplished by considering alternative ways to reflect on and to measure one's behaviors.
- Efficiency and effectiveness are only two of many criteria one can use for measuring progress toward goals.
- Other criteria can also be used to measure and develop goals that bring well-being to the individuals in the group.
- Growth mindset is a measure that can be used to track one's growth in psychosocial skills, just as the Bhutanese use GNH to measure their country's growth.
- You can use your growth mindset to lead others to growth.
- Wisdom is associated with the integration of previously acquired knowledge.
- Self-reflection is necessary to correct errors in knowledge structures and develop transcendent values (beyond self-interest).

Chapter 9

Norms and Organizing

In a real sense all life is inter-related. All men are caught in an inescapable network of mutuality, tied in a single garment of destiny. Whatever affects one directly affects all indirectly. I can never be what I ought to be until you are what you ought to be, and you can never be what you ought to be until I am what I ought to be. . . . This is the inter-related structure of reality.

—Martin Luther King Jr., *Letter from Birmingham Jail:*
Martin Luther King Jr.'s Letter from Birmingham Jail and the
Struggle That Changed a Nation

Individuals come together and create organizations because they have a need for support to meet their personal goals. When group behavior is healthy, there exist clear social norms. Healthy organizations have embedded procedural and organizational justice processes into the formal systems. Transcendent moral referents provide a moral compass, or collective consciousness, that empowers individuals to act in alignment with their values (Milgram, 1986).

Rawls (1985) described the use of moral values as a necessary component of social order that includes "a moral conception worked out for a specific kind of subject, namely, for political, social, and economic institutions . . . to apply to . . . the "basic structure" of a modern constitutional democracy" (p. 224).

A critical feature of open systems is the flexibility to adapt to changes where needed resulting in individual and organizational vitality. Empirically, evidence has suggested we can understand and support the creation of healthy system structures by focusing on three areas: leadership, formal system structures, and informal social relational structures (Hanson, 2015).

FORMAL SYSTEM VERSUS SOCIAL ORGANIZING

Systems are needed to order and direct behaviors and resources in all human activities. Formal systems are made up of processes, established procedures, rules, and regulations that define the *formal* relationships and order the behaviors of individuals in the system through the power of their external structures. Formal systems are a part of society and embedded in *institutions* such as churches, universities, hospitals, marriage, corporations, and legislative bodies.

Leaders within systems have proxy agency power to represent the individuals in the system. Lacking transcendent standards, some systems may sanction amoral behaviors to meet political or market goals, to the detriment of those in the system and in society (Bandura, 2002; Tarter and Hoy, 2004).

Politics

Politics can be defined as those actions of individuals, who seek to control, or influence, the resources and decisions of the group. Political action can be either legitimate or illegitimate. Legitimate political activity seeks to meet the needs of the collective and bring the organization further toward it goals (Mintzberg, 1983; Tarter and Hoy, 2004). When political actions have illegitimate goals, they are neither supported by the explicit goals of the group nor acting as proxy to represent the needs of the collective.

It is impossible to have a healthy organization without moral values embedded in the norms of the systems, institutions, leadership, and processes. Healthy organizations with healthy social norms and aligned goals may still become subverted through informal hierarchies, with political agendas serving illegitimate goals. Institutions can benefit the individuals they influence, or they can be controlled by a minority of individuals and directed to benefit a few.

For example, Glattfelder (2013) explained that in the current world economies only "737 top shareholders have the potential to collectively control 80 percent of the [transnational corporations'] value. . . . [T]hese 737 top players make up a bit more than 0.1 percent [of the total players]" (10:23). Only 146 shareholders at the center of this economic system control 40 percent of all TNC's value. This was possible due to a high level of interconnectivity between these individuals and insulation of influence from others (Peralta, 2013; Vitali, Glattfelder, and Battiston, 2011, p. e25995).

Rule of Law

Legal codes and sanctions are developed within and between groups, such as in a society, and include how the society will regulate relationships between people(s) and legal entities. The purpose of governance is to identify when and how legitimate force can be used to restrict or control behavior. MacIver in Bierstedt (1981) wrote, "Force, when rightly used, is the servant of liberty. It is the *ultima ratio* of society" (p. 266).

Time has shown that stronger individuals, or groups of individuals, directing the resources and decisions of legal entities such as corporations, may overreach those commanding fewer resources. A healthy society can be maintained only when the rule of law is followed equitably for all, using proxy agency to advocate for the protection of the less financially resourced and society as a whole.

An imbalance in monetary/economic resources is inevitable while the majority of individuals operate under social norms seeking the welfare of others and not a monetary advantage in their exchanges; while some fewer individuals rise to scale level advantages using socially unaccountable market norms. Again, recall that values are used as criteria for judging actions and policies, and often are conflicting.

Vital leadership with wisdom to navigate the consequences of economic policies and their effects on social well-being is one of the three cornerstones available to leverage improvements and stability in the social order.

Unhealthy Use of Law/Force

The misuse of the law can be easily discerned. Recourse to enforce one's goals through use of the law should be the "last resort," used for purposes of advancing the overall liberty in a society when moral conscious is not present to regulate behaviors. A healthy society uses legal processes that increase the ability of the individuals and the group in society to function and maintain liberty.

When powerful personal interest groups use the law to gain more power and take advantage of the less advantaged, or disrupt ethical processes, an unhealthy system is the result. The preferred means to ensuring a healthy social order is to embed transcendent values as social norms into the formal system structures.

Force is not to be considered as an expedient means for ensuring power and profit at the expense of society's other members, who have less financial, political, or relational resources. Legal and police force has limited long-term value in ensuring healthy human societies (Bierstedt, 1981).

INFORMAL STRUCTURES—THE CONCEPT OF ORGANIZING

So how do we know when individuals are organized versus strictly operating within a formal structure and not creating healthy social relationships?

MacIver in Bierstedt (1981) explained that when individuals develop understandings of common expected behaviors, or *norms,* this is evidence that the individuals are acknowledging one another and agreeing on expectations, that is, they are organizing. This then becomes the glue between the individual's inner and outer environment.

He explained,

> In so far as the social order reflects the common interests of men, which must be shared in order to be realized, the individual is both free within, and sustained in his individuality, by society. In this situation he is able to say, "we' instead of merely "I" . . . (p. 268)

Recall that norms are social rules that govern the behaviors in the organization. Norms develop an understanding between individuals they belong to something outside of themselves. Groups create behavioral obligations, with social consequences, to ensure compliance if the group norms are broken (Lewis, 1969). We increase the predictability of the group and signal to others we can be trusted to act as expected when we perform according to the given norms of a group.

Some behaviors can break down the development of community. Divisive behaviors are those that stem from individuals seeking to control the decisions and resources, including the time, of the group for personal goals rather than aligning personal and group goals. In these cases the group may employ a formal, or informal, sanction or consequence such as calling attention to the behavior and redirecting the offending persons.

Identification with an In-Group

In-groups are formed when individuals participate in normed behaviors and take on a common social identity. In-group members receive the protection and benefits of group membership. Out-group members do not (Young, 2008). In prior cultures, such as Babylon, the ruler's power and prestige was increased by supporting the arts and creative expression to develop a collective cultural awareness.

In today's twenty-first-century technological world, a variety of voices have the power to speak to the people in order to develop collective understandings. Researchers have found that through the influence of mass media individuals are identifying with and acting collectively with the out-group and more individualistically, or independently, within the historical in-groups.

One can realize how influential one can become using media influences that redirect the transmission of values from between in-group members, such as family and faith groups, to the out-group. With technological communications, out-group members' histories and agendas (where they are from and where they are going) may be largely unknown to the individual viewers or listeners.

This can occur because social media and the influence of fast fashion (inexpensive and quickly changing products) can give the impression of social identification. That is, a false sense of connection and trust can develop through frequent exposure to media over time without having face-to-face experiences that determine if the out-group agenda is safe.

Factioning versus Aligning Goals

External influences, such as media and marketing, may generate factions. When individuals assert themselves and their personal views at the expense of peace and unity within their in-groups (such as with family, friends, co-workers, or school groups) the result is "factioning." Factioning breaks down the collective efficacy of existing in-group members and prevents progress toward creating broader safe and healthy connections through expanding social identification and aligning goals.

Factioning can be overcome by making explicit the implicit goals and agendas of those with whom one is identifying. Strong vital leadership is necessary to develop system structures that unite individuals and provide predictability and stability. Individuals develop trust when they feel they are supported, not left alone to defend themselves in challenging organizational situations.

Individual perceptions of organizational justice within the work context support taking risks and participating in informal activities beyond the formal roles. Developing positive social relational networks, shared meanings, and social identities requires individuals to spend time together and develop collaboration (Hanson, 2015; Niqab et al., in process).

NORMS

Norms provide opportunities for members to demonstrate their willingness to identify with and integrate into the group. Two types of norms will be discussed here, social and market (economic) norms. Recall the algorithms that provide guidance for birds to flock in synchrony; they were able to avoid dangers and respond to each other's movements. This compares favorably to the concept of social norms which solidify the group by

- coordinating complex activities;
- reducing the cost of social transactions;
- saving time in constant debate over what is expected;
- setting standards of behavior to be used to resolve disagreements (Young, 2008).

Social norms and market norms are mutually exclusive. Most people work for more than a paycheck. Individuals gain meaning in their lives from making a social contribution and by developing a social identity through their roles and the tasks they perform. Three methods of implementing and maintaining norms will be discussed: coordination, social disapproval, and internalization.

Implementing and Maintaining Norms

Coordination

Individuals willingly conform to norms that increase the coordination of the group, such as everyone agreeing to drive on the right side of the road to prevent collisions. Either side works as long as everyone on the same road conforms to the norm for that area (Young, 2008).

Social Disapproval

The basis for some norms can't be easily recognized. Some are developed by chance, or arbitrarily over time, as a response to solving a problem. Once established, the expected behavior stays in place due to the group seeing the norm as "right" or necessary. Violation of the norm triggers sanctions of disapproval (Young, 2008).

Internalization

When an individual internalizes a norm, enforcement is self-imposed. An individual violating the norm may feel a sense of shame or guilt. When individuals internalize expected behaviors of the group, they perform the normative behavior even when no one sees. An example might be not littering, or tipping a waiter an expected percentage for good service (Kahneman, 2011).

Social Norms

Social norms are behaviors that relate to the development of one's individual and social identities. They build expectations for how to act within the group relationships. Individuals are willing to go above and beyond their normal work roles when they receive social recognition and support and feel valued. Behaviors such as organizational citizenship result from the individuals integrating the social norms of a healthy group (DeGroot and Brownlee, 2006; Niqab et al., in process).

Organizational Citizenship Behaviors (OCB)

Examples of organizational citizenship behaviors include staying late to complete an important task without expecting extra pay, helping a coworker understand the expectations of a job, and standing up for the company when others criticize. When individuals receive benefits of support and caring from their relationships on the job, they respond by recognizing and supporting the immediate needs of the individuals and organization in the context.

Counterproductive Work Behaviors (CWB)

When the workload or organizational procedures are not equitable and just, such as when only a few individuals are exhibiting OCB, then CWB may occur. For example, in some institutions where most employees operate under market norms and don't contribute beyond their contracted duties, others may take on extra work to keep things running. Resentments can build up, and the same employees going above and beyond might then exhibit CWB.

Individuals may express their feelings of resentment and negativity on the job, not help others when they are able to do so, and suffer from overwork and negative consequences in their private lives. Leaders in organizations need to be aware of how to protect individuals from imbalances in OCB by holding individuals equally accountable for work performance.

OCB, in organizations, compares similarly to the concept of an organizational level growth mindset culture, including processes of supportive leadership, collaborative problem solving, and civic virtue (Niqab et al., in process). Hierarchical structure and separation of certain formal functions are necessary to provide the structure for healthy social organizing (interconnectivity of the members).

Informal Structures

A healthy social order includes social norms demonstrated in its customs, religious and legal codes, moral standards, and agreed-upon social ways of behaving and thinking (Bierstedt, 1981). When healthy informal structures are in place, all individuals share in the development of new knowledge and influence the collective behaviors, such as the creation of new norms.

Informal structures result from the social relationships that develop between individuals. The informal structure includes patterns in the relationships (who talks to whom and when), the quality of relationships (built on trust or not), and the power relationships (ability to share and create new knowledge) (Bolino, Turnley, and Bloodgood, 2002).

Market Norms

Under market conditions, economic (monetary) values take priority over social values. Personal caring and social relationship are not expected under market norms of equitable exchange (Ariely, 2008). Market norms do not have an inherent social function other than the immediate expectation of receiving a reciprocal benefit, such as employees expecting equal and immediate return for the work they do in the form of a paycheck for hours worked (Carlin and Love, 2013).

Market norms take precedence when monetary values are placed on performance. Paying someone to do the right thing has been shown to have a counterproductive effect. Cognitive processes take over, and the individual acts according to market (economic) norms rather than social norms.

For example, making incentive payments to teachers for high classroom outcomes on accountability tests would establish market norms in school systems that "normally' operate under social norms to produce social connection and student development. Research suggests incentive pay for teachers would reduce the development of collective efficacy and ultimately reduce organizational outcomes (Kahneman, 2011).

Market Norms, Fraud, and Greed

Market norms may place employees at a tremendous disadvantage if ethical considerations are not considered. Bandura (2001) wrote, "Social bonds and communal commitments that lack marketability are especially vulnerable to erosion by global market forces unfettered by social obligation" (p. 17).

University of California at Berkeley psychologist Paul Piff explained,

> We've been finding that wealthy individuals are more likely to perceive the pursuit of self-interest as opposed to the collective interest as being moral and favorable. We're even observing this moralization of greed. This greed is good mentality. (Round, 2015)

Amoral systems operate on market or political agendas. Kahneman (2011) wrote that humans are easily exploited by "an unscrupulous firm" (pp. 269 and 413). Systems and institutions are not people and require explicit actions of the leaders and collective to embed social norms into the structures and rituals.

Round (2015) explained

> It's the institutions that prioritize getting ahead above all else; that it's OK to break the law if that means you are going to make more profits for the company with no attention to what the consequences are for the system as a whole.

Large corporate fraud has resulted when, usually honest people, model unethical behaviors of coworkers and superiors operating under market norms (Ariely, 2012). Economic motives are not informed by transcendent moral values that consider the effects of one's actions on self, others, the earth, and spiritual considerations.

Gandhi (in Attenborough, 1982) said

> The economics that disregard moral and sentimental considerations are like wax works that being life-like still lack the life of the living flesh. At every crucial moment these newfangled economic laws have broken down in practice. And nations or individuals who accept them as guiding maxims must perish. (p. 30)

Priming the Context

Many people are aware of the priming influence of marketing images, the use of music in advertising to influence one's emotions, and even political media campaigns designed to direct voting behaviors. Many individuals in society are aware of the processes of language and the influence speech and images have on individual thought and behaviors. Chomsky, in Round (2015), explained,

> If you take an economics course, you are taught that markets are based on informed consumers making rational judgments. But suppose you turn on the television set and take a look at the ads. Now are they trying to create informed consumers making rational choices? On the contrary, they are trying to create uninformed consumers, who will act irrationally. And it's a huge industry. One of the biggest industries in the country.

Consider how images and language used in the social media, mass media, music, the marketplace, and your social context influence your mindset both consciously and subconsciously. A statement made in the film *The Divide* encouraged collective action to facilitate healthy systems, institutions, and social organization, "The feeling that there is some mechanism out there about which you can do nothing at all, that's simply not true. If people want to change this they can change it" (Round, 2015).

Developing an understanding of how the processes of organizing occur increases your power of personal choice and the ability to maintain the integrity of your actions with your values; while operating within systems that may not reflect common accepted social norms developed using transcendent referents.

The Silver Lining between Social and Market Norms

The difference between social norms and market norms may be understood by an analogy of a mirror. Early civilizations, as far back as the Roman Empire, used mirrors. The process for creating high quality mirrors wasn't perfected until around the sixteenth century and was called "silvering." The skills required to perform the art included applying a uniform thin metallic coating to a high-quality, defect-free plate of clear glass ("History of Glass," 2012).

An individual looking through a sheet of clear glass has a view of the world and others without obstruction. However, once the glass has been "silvered," the viewer's ability to see through the glass to the other side is blocked. One's attention is directed back to the self. Even an individual with, metaphorically speaking, no imperfections may be influenced to focus on personal advantage at the expense of others when operating under conditions of market norms and in systems where greed is modeled and moral standards and account-ability are lacking.

Leadership Style and Norms

Transformational leaders elicit *social norms* to raise others to higher morali-ties and motivation for causes that are valuable to the individual participants (Kouzes and Posner, 2007, p. 22). *Transactional* leaders use *market norms* of mutually beneficial exchanges between leader and follower. Transactional leaders set the performance expectations so the workers understand the expectations of the exchange. For example, a transactional leader provides wages and benefits in exchange for the followers work efforts (Den Hartog, Van Muijen, and Koopman, 1997).

INDIVIDUAL AGENCY AND SOCIAL INTEGRATION

Albert Bandura (2001) explained, "Human functioning is rooted in social systems." The structure of a system is a model of reciprocal causality and "a dynamic interplay between individuals and those who preside over the insti-tutionalized operations of social systems" (p. 15). Barley (1994) in Bandura (2001) wrote, "People achieve the greatest personal efficacy and productivity when their psychological orientation is congruent with the structure of the social system" (p. 17).

Dr. Alden Cass (1999), a clinical psychologist known for helping Wall Street stockbrokers, shared his findings that a crisis in connected social relationships was occurring (Round, 2015). Cass's findings highlighted the importance of developing psychosocial skills through social-relational norms for healthy organizing where you live and work.

The structure of systems influences the individuals operating under their rules through the authority of the leader, who has power to hold them accountable. However, the formal system and the psychological qualities of the individuals within the systems are not divided into discrete and separate components. There exists an interplay between individual agency and collective agency that can shape the group's environment for the betterment of all.

The Power of Personal Choice

As human beings we are not perfect. We sometimes miscommunicate and misunderstand, or sometimes just act badly. Developing one's power of personal choice provides one with the ability to respond flexibly to changing circumstances, so one can "land on the ship's deck instead of in the water." Individuals need to learn discernment, boundary setting, forgiveness, and bonding in social relationships. Flexibility is the ability to choose effective responses that are just right for the situation at hand. Developing resilience through the use of discernment is the way one keeps in integrity with one's values, while maintaining boundaries and developing healthy relationships in a social environment.

Discernment

Discernment is the ability to recognize what to share and what not to share, and when to engage and when not to engage. We must learn to give to the group what is necessary for successfully working together. It is not wise to entrust all of oneself to any group or individual. Philippe Petit (2014), the creative artist, who walked between the twin towers on a high wire, explained in his book, *Creativity, the Perfect Crime,* that, in order to survive, one must keep a sense of humor and remain secretive.

Secretive in this context refers to discernment. Learning discernment includes choosing how to present oneself to the group in ways that protect oneself from the few who might take advantage. Individuals can learn to exhibit those behaviors we observe that work well and eliminate behaviors that do not.

For example, children need to be told that, though they don't have the right to criticize an adult's behavior, they do have permission to watch the adults in their world and decide which of the adult behaviors are working and worthwhile to use in their own lives. However, if an adult's behavior does not seem to be working well, the child should be free to choose not to engage in that behavior and to avoid situations where others use it, such as misuse of alcohol or drugs, unsafe driving, or emotionally unsafe speaking.

It is critical for individuals to build skills for choosing healthy personal behaviors and selecting healthy social relationships. The process of observing others' perform skills successfully and copying them is termed *modeling* and was described by Bandura (2001) in his social cognitive theory. Leaders can model a belief in growth so individuals feel supported for the development of a growth mindset.

You can maximize your power of personal choice and avoid embedding yourself in hurtful behaviors of self and others by managing your mindset. No one has to be stuck with behaviors that don't work, even when we see others stuck in them. Reflecting on the usefulness of our own behaviors and others promotes autonomy through the use of critical thinking skills and discernment.

When you leave the organization and go home, you are your own person with special skills, values, beliefs, hopes, and goals. You are free to learn skills and grow in ways that maximize your personal power of choice for healthy human well-being. The complexity and unpredictability of our behavior is part of being human. The flexibility provided by resilience and discernment can empower an individual to adjust his or her choices under stress conditions, resolve conflicts, and maintain consistency with his or her personal values and goals.

Resilience

Resilience is a skill one develops that includes discernment of when to pull back from a situation or relationship for safety. That's not all. To be resilient one must learn how to re-engage when a situation is emotionally and physically safe. The ability to recognize when a situation is physically, socially, and emotionally safe and how to connect, disconnect, and reengage has historically developed during childhood.

Healthy parents, school systems (teachers), and community members provide scaffolding and modeling. Flexibility results in the ability to be resilient and is often demonstrated by individuals and groups with growth mindset beliefs. Resilience is the result of a strong personal and social identity, intrinsic locus of control, self-efficacy, and personal ability to regulate one's emotions (Ng et al., 2006).

Self-Image

An individual's *self-image* develops through feedback from a variety of sources; internal, external, social, and transcendent. What you think and believe about yourself directly influences your feelings, physiology, and indirectly the choices you make. One's perceptions of control over his or her environment directly relates to one's evaluations of self-worth. The idea of self-evaluation is derived from four psychological inputs: one's sense of control, self-esteem, self-efficacy, and emotional stability (Ng, Sorensen, and Eby, 2006).

A transcendent self-awareness through reflection on transcendent norms increases one's power of personal choice, which is required to maintain a flexible balance between the individual self and one's social identity. Discernment and wisdom give one the ability to manage the visceral (self-centered) nature.

Key points to remember

- The way we organize with others influences our relationships and how we choose to act.
- The memories we create of our interactions with others result in the concept of the organization and develop the expected norms of our collective behaviors.
- Healthy organizing requires the development of social identities by the individuals in the group.
- Social and market/economic norms contribute to different expected behaviors in the group.
- Social norms promote trust when individuals comply with the expected group behaviors though one must be discerning to avoid over exposing oneself when interacting with others who operate under market norms.
- Under market norms, individuals expect immediate reciprocal benefits and this reduces individual willingness to go above and beyond when the situation requires individual choice to help out.
- Under market norm conditions, individuals may model others' behaviors of greed leading to fraud and theft.
- All systems are not equal. Where collective efficacy does not develop, the system may be amoral.

Chapter 10

Understanding Your Behaviors in the Group

Coming together is the beginning. Keeping together is progress. Working together is success.

—Henry Ford

Did you know researchers developed many of the behavior management strategies used today from studies on the behaviors of animals? You may have heard of a well-known learning process called Pavlovian conditioning: demonstrated by training dogs to salivate when they heard a bell ring. Many teachers use classroom discipline management plans based on this same *conditioning by association* of a stimulus and a reward (Jozefowiez, 2014).

In the twentieth century, researchers performed experimental studies observing the behaviors of animals in attempts to develop theories of human learning. This type of research was called behaviorism. Behaviorist theories excluded the study of one's personal choice on one's behavior, considering it unscientific because the processes of the mind were unseen and therefore difficult to measure.

However, Sociologist William Bruce Cameron (1963) understood the importance of studying unseen influences when he stated,

It would be nice if all of the data which sociologists require could be enumerated because then we could run them through IBM machines and draw charts as the economists do. However, not everything that can be counted counts, and not everything that counts can be counted. (p. 13)

Pink (2009) challenged behaviorist models of management saying, "Traditional notions of management are great if you want compliance. But if you want engagement, self-direction works better" (12:58). Today, organizational theorists have begun to understand the importance of studying psychological and social influences on human motivation that result from the organizational structures in which we live, work, and play.

A review of the literature identifies three important elements of human motivation:

- Autonomy: a balance between independence and social integration, alignment of one's tasks with personal values
- Mastery: the desire to get better and better at something that matters, including repeated practice over time resulting in transferable learning
- Purpose: the yearning to do what we do in the service of something larger than ourselves, social contribution, and transcendent self-awareness (Hanson, 2015; Pink, 2009, 12:17)

Bandura (2001) explained the importance of human social interactions on one's sense of autonomy, learning, and motivation when he advanced the theory of social cognitive learning. Bandura described three primary ways people can act autonomously in the world; through individual agency, proxy agency, and collective agency.

MINDSET AND AGENCY

The concept of a growth mindset is situated in the framework of social cognitive theory (Bandura, 1977; Dweck, 1986, 1989). Students with growth mindsets have been shown to display improved academic behaviors, have higher motivation, and choose more challenging goals than students reporting fixed mindset beliefs (Blackwell, Trzesniewski, and Dweck, 2007; Farrington et al., 2012).

Individual Agency and Efficacy

Agency is the ability to act. Recall how learning creates patterns in the brain for the purpose of taking action. Social cognitive theory describes personal agency as the ability to "make things happen by one's own actions" (Bandura, 2001, pp. 1 and 2). One's efficacy, belief in the ability to be successful by one's actions, is a key to social cognitive theory. Efficacy beliefs influence one's openness to engage new learning and to persist through challenges.

Self-efficacy (SE) is one's belief that one's actions are responsible for the success of one's future outcomes and the belief one will be successful at new experiences (Bandura, 1994). SE contributes to one's personal and social skills and results, in part, from a sense of belonging in the group, power in one's social relationships, relevance of tasks required of them, and one's belief in the ability to grow through effort (Hanson, 2017b). Individuals can feel self-efficacy in one area and not another; that means SE is *context dependent*, as is growth mindset.

Individuals organize because they have a need for increased efficacy through collective action. However, to be successful working in groups requires a high level of cognitive development; because of the complexity of interacting with diverse others; and the necessity of behaving in ways that consider the needs and well-being of others, not just the self. When participation in groups goes well, individuals increase their sense of efficacy through the following ways;

- developing successful skills (mastery experiences);
- seeing others perform skills successfully (vicarious experiences);
- being told one can be successful (social persuasion);
- learning the ability to manage one's emotions and stress (arousal) (Bandura, 1989b).

Proxy Agency

Proxy agency occurs when one person acts in behalf of another to obtain resources and to manage the social environment. A proxy agent has skills, resources, social capital, and power to help another person. Individuals seek a proxy when they are unable, or unwilling, to reach their goals alone. Most individuals prefer to get help from others to reach their goals than to exclusively act independently using their own agency.

The use of proxy agency contributes to the advantages we receive through the division of labor and specialization. The use of proxy is evident in living organisms and in human systems; increases efficiencies; and provides advantages to both the group and individuals. Vital leaders act as proxy agents when they demonstrate procedural justice and make ethical decisions for the group, leading to trust and collective efficacy.

Collective Agency

Collective agency "is the group's belief in its collective ability to act effectively to represent the individuals' goals." Collective agency is a result of the collective and independent actions of the individuals in the group. Bandura (2001, 2011) warned it is *vital* that individuals be aware and act with collective agency. We must recognize the role individual agency, proxy agency, and collective agency have in shaping the world, through just and equitable processes, for the protection and well-being of all.

COLLECTION VERSUS COLLECTIVE

Individuals participate in many groups and organizations, hopefully for the mutual benefit of all involved. A primary result of healthy human social organization is the creation of common meaning together that will generate a greater benefit to the individuals, and group, than the individuals could accomplish alone. Certain conditions must exist for a group of individuals to become an organization capable of collective action.

Individual and organizational well-being results from flexibility, feelings of belonging, social contribution, and trust. No single group or organization can supply all the needs of the individuals. Individuals must develop the ability to recognize when to assert their individual versus their social identity to maintain a sense of healthy autonomy. This means learning skills to adapt and shape our collective responses in a complex world (Bandura, 2001, 2011; Burnette, O'Boyle, Vanepps, Pollack, and Finkel, 2013; Collinson and Cook, 2007; Dweck, 2012; Hong, Chiu, Dweck, and Sacks, 1997; Novak, 2002; Senge, 1990).

Your task will be to identify whether the individuals in your group(s) act as a collection or a collective. Is the group organized for healthy collective action with a mindset founded in moral agency and common social norms?

Concept of the Collective

Social scientists have argued over the meaning of society and the concept of a collective. A key point of contention is whether the group is an entity in its own right. The reason this is important is that if the abstract concept is given "thing" status, there is a danger that the idea may take precedence over the individual. Bandura emphasized that though the individual may act in a group setting, the sum of the individuals does not make a separate thing that becomes greater than the parts.

Rather, a healthy organization is evidenced by the collective benefit provided by the group to the well-being of the individuals. MacIver (1949) in Bierstedt (1981), an eminent social scientist and major contributor to the development of the field of sociology, described the group social concept stating, "[T]here are no individuals who are not social individuals, and society is nothing more than individuals associated and organized" (p. 254).

Identity–Individual, Team/Group, Organizational, Symbolic, and Transformative

One's identity develops on several levels and begins in childhood. Initially, the self-identity is formed through relationship with family, friends, and close others, who are responsible for one's welfare and development. As the child grows through scaffolding by the family, a healthy self-identity develops. Children develop cognitive skills that extend their abilities for participating in small groups such as athletic teams, clubs, and personal interest groups.

With positive team identities and recognition for one's progressing personal skills and contribution, the expanding sense of self forms into a social identity. Additional identities include one's organizational involvement, workplace identity, extended family, country of origin, and cross-cultural experiences, if the individual has opportunities to immerse in other cultural worlds.

As one matures, the transcendent self-awareness and identity follows. Leaders with vital awareness demonstrate qualities which are evidenced by their wisdom and trustworthiness. This gradual development and expansion of one's sense of self compares favorably with Bandura's (1989c), Maslow's (1954), and Piaget's (1958) explanations of human psychological growth.

An example of an individual's expansion of self-identity is provided in a study performed with kidney donors. Researchers interviewed individuals, who had donated a kidney to a stranger. They wanted to know what made them different from others who did not donate kidneys. Most donors answered that they were the same as everyone else. The donors' level of connection with others' needs was extremely high and their sense of self was extremely humble (Marsh, 2016).

Individual Mindset in the Group Context

Dweck hypothesized that how people display themselves in a group is influenced by the individuals' need to be valued and accepted. Researchers explored the influence of the organization on the individual's beliefs, behaviors, and motivation (Murphy and Dweck, 2010). As briefly discussed in another section, results showed that individuals tended to conform in their behaviors to the normed beliefs of the group; that is, individuals took on growth mindsets when in a group with a growth mindset culture (Delaney, Dweck, Murphy, Chatman, and Kray, 2015).

School administrators and business managers can influence followers' individual mindset beliefs indirectly by working to develop systems that support growth mindset cultures in schools and businesses.

Collecting individual mindset survey data is useful to begin conversations with

- students about how one's brain can grow through one's being open to learn and by putting in effort (engaging);
- teachers about how their mindset beliefs have been shown to explain differences in the teaching strategies they use and their behaviors toward students that influence student outcomes;

- leaders about how their mindset beliefs can affect their followers' trust in them and willingness to follow (Dweck, 2002; Farrington et al., 2012; Heslin, Vanderwalle, and Latham, 2007).

Caveat: Remember, as just described, when measuring individuals' mindset beliefs, the individual beliefs do not sum and average to the group's belief; even though the individuals may take on the beliefs of the group temporarily while working in them (Hanson, Bangert, and Ruff, 2016).

ORGANIZATIONAL MINDSET BEHAVIORS

Researchers collaborated on a two-year study to perform interviews and to survey employees in Fortune 1000 companies. Organizational mindset was shown to be the key factor in developing positive behaviors within the organization. These behaviors included resilience, innovation, collaboration, engagement, commitment, and trust (Delaney, Dweck, Murphy, Chatman, and Kray, 2015).

In another study, the organization's fixed versus growth mindset view of intelligence affected the individuals' self-perceptions, motivation, and behavior toward others. This agrees with previous studies that group-level mindset theories influenced the way people in the group perceived what the organization valued (Delaney, Dweck, Murphy, Chatman, and Kray, 2015; Murphy and Dweck, 2010).

The following list describes the reciprocal influence the organization has on

- how individuals displayed themselves to the group to gain acceptance and avoid negative judgment;
- how the individuals' values changed as they internalized the group values;
- how the individuals in the group later evaluated themselves and evaluated and treated others in unrelated contexts;
- how the individuals made their choice of goals;
- the level of persistence they displayed in the face of challenge;
- their level of collaboration with others (Murphy and Dweck, 2010).

Organizational growth mindset cultures build from the shared norms and behaviors of the group and their reciprocal influence on the individuals. Developing systems within the organization, and teaching individuals how to collaborate and communicate, are the primary strategies a leader can use to ensure collaborative sense making occurs. The development of a growth mindset contributes to the development of the collective efficacy of the group (Burcharth and Fosfuri, 2015; Hanson, Ruff, and Bangert, 2016).

The central goal of all organizing is to make sense of a complex world in ways that the group supports the abilities of the individuals to adapt and grow. Note there is a difference between decision making and sense making.

Decision making is developing predictions and testing them in order to identify successful plans for acting toward one's goals.

Sense making, in an organization, is for the purpose of developing new knowledge to adapt to changing circumstances in the complex environment in which it operates and occurs through relational learning empowering individuals to share their expertise (Courtney, Navarro, and O'Hare, 2007).

New United Motor Manufacturing, Inc. (NUMMI)

This section gives insights into how a failing GM plant was able to transform to the highly successful New United Motor Manufacturing, Inc. (NUMMI) using the same management and workforce. In the 1980s General Motors (GM) automobile manufacturing company had significant issues with its manufacturing plants. In particular, a plant in Fremont, California, was considered for shutdown due to serious conflicts between management and employees that undermined productivity in the workplace.

The individuals were motivated to change. If the plant shut down, they were going to lose their jobs. An engineer went to study the automobile manufacturing process in Japan in an effort to find a solution. He brought back a method of teamwork he observed used in the Toyota automobile manufacturing plants. GM agreed to implement the changes in the plant and sent a group of willing employees to Japan to learn the processes.

What happened when they returned was a revolution in plant culture that turned the plant around and made it one of the most successful facilities in the corporation (Wilms, Hardcastle, and Zell, 1994). First, everyone had to be open to learn; willing to overcome the challenges that routinely occur in communicating with others. During the startup, everyone in the workplace developed new mindsets, the belief that they all could grow and learn new ways of doing things.

The plant managers learned how to demonstrate they could be trusted and gave assurances that working together would benefit all involved. They established predictable and stable routines for running the day-to-day operations that supported the workers in their ability to do the job successfully.

The workers sought to regain the managers' trust. The individuals made real commitments to no longer disrupt the operations. Employees were able to engage in successful dialogue with management, and develop supportive teams and skills to perform the new processes. Participation, mutual respect, and trust were required for developing new outcomes (Courtney, Navarro, and O'Hare, 2007).

NUMMI learned new ways of operating; that is, the group developed new social norms for behaviors that all were willing to perform. The new social norms provided new identities to the workers, increased the group's trust, and developed collective efficacy through acting on a belief in their ability to grow and learn together. A growth mindset culture developed.

Caveat. The new management and processes that worked at NUMMI did not transfer to other plants at GM. This is evidence that learning is an individualized proposition and requires an openness to change, personal autonomous choice to engage, and supportive leadership.

LEADERSHIP WITHIN OPEN VITAL SYSTEMS

Albert Bandura (2001) declared, "Human functioning is rooted in social systems." He explained the reciprocal influence that the structure of a system has on the individuals as "a dynamic interplay between individuals and those who preside over the institutionalized operations of social systems" (p. 15). The key element influencing the improvement of individuals and organizations is *this interplay* between the two.

Developing healthy organizations requires more than individuals coming together. A framework, or theory of mind, must be established through which to view the world. As we develop our understandings together, new language is developed to communicate the meanings in the context of our social situations. For example, the framework for a growth mindset and collective efficacy can be viewed through social cognitive theory and open systems (Dweck, 2010; Hanson, 2015; Hoy, Tarter and Kottkamp, 1991; Senge, 1990 and 2006; Tarter and Hoy, 2004).

Leadership within open vital systems is set within the theoretical framework developed in this book and is named here *social cognitive vital awareness*. The following discussion briefly reviews the processes and structures used in developing leadership within open vital systems in your family, school, organization, team, or group.

Open Systems

von Bertalanffy (1968) developed the general systems theory and explained the difference between open and closed systems. He proposed the idea of self-organizing in open systems that leads to the development of teams and shared leadership. An open system is evidenced by an overall *vitality* of the organization (Boulding, n.d., para. 13). (Recall how the hydra developed.)

Open systems promote feelings of purpose within members by providing opportunities for social contribution (giving of oneself for the benefit of others) and increase the sharing of knowledge and creation of shared meaning. Learning occurs in an organization when the leaders and individuals work together and are able to respond flexibly to challenges, and to make adjustments in the system that brings vitality.

Remember, individuals must have high skills to perform their jobs and to self-regulate (to do no harm to others) in a social context that allows flexibility in systems, laws, and hierarchies. The greater the differentiation of tasks and diversity of backgrounds between individuals within the social context, the greater will be the need for social education, beyond just the training in skills necessary for task performance (MacIver, 1917, p. 306).

Where skills are lacking, increased hierarchical structure and formal leadership is necessary to ensure equitable processes, supervision, and direction of the workplace tasks and behaviors. Recall the skills described throughout this book including understanding the theories of mind and the ability to present oneself socially (social education), supported by the development of vital awareness.

Individuals develop a vital awareness as they demonstrate the abilities to reflect, correct errors in assumptions, challenge one's prior thinking, develop an expanding social identity, and humility. Social norms provide a safe environment for individuals to develop skills to do the job. Encouragement to risk failure and allowing sufficient time and supports ensures the cyclical stages of practice toward mastering new skills will occur.

Vital leadership (VL)

Leadership is necessary within systems to provide structure, stability, and predictability, and solve system issues that go beyond the power and influence of individuals within them. The leader's formal hierarchical role provides power which can be used in proxy agency to represent and meet the needs of the members.

Boomer (2014) described three distinct roles of formal authority in systems including leading, managing, and administering. The first relates to vision and planning at the system level, the second to execution of and creating value on a daily basis, and the last overseeing and ensuring accomplishment of the assigned tasks and processes (para. 1).

Vital leadership, within the context of LOVS, is described as operating through two modes: a transformational and a managerial (Niqab, et al., in process).

Transformational leaders promote the development of social norms, direct members to reflect and use high standards as guides, and unify the collective through holding the common vision before the group (Kouzes and Posner, 2007, p. 22).

Managerial leadership is the power of the leader to make decisions related to the physical elements of the system and with regard to the employee roles and behaviors within the system (such as managing personnel, providing trainings, allocating time and physical resources for individuals to work and plan together).

Vital leaders use the processes of pacing and leading to elicit their followers' cooperation. This includes social identification, use of hierarchical authority, an awareness in the leader of a system's perspective, and the ability to anticipate dangers and to obtain cooperation from one's subordinates to follow the leader to avoid them. The analogy of a highway patrol officer can be used to help understand these processes.

If someone asked you to go out on a busy freeway where traffic is flowing in five lanes at a speed of 70 mph and to stop the traffic, what would you say? Highway patrol officers do this regularly. For example, situations arise where debris falls onto the highway and must be removed. In order to get the clean-up equipment onto the highway, and a safe space for workers to pick it up, the traffic must be slowed and routed around the debris. How does the highway patrol officer get the traffic to stop?

First the patrol officer enters the freeway far below the danger spot. The officer flows into the traffic at the speed the others are going (pacing). The officer then turns on the patrol car vehicle warning lights and begins to weave back and forth across the freeway lanes, while slowing the speed of the patrol car. The other drivers respond to the flashing lights and the weaving patrol car and slow their speed accordingly.

When the officer sees the traffic has slowed in all lanes, he begins to lead the cars. The drivers follow the officer's vehicle going forward at a safe speed. By the time they arrive to the danger spot, the drivers are able to discern how to avoid the debris. The highway workers are safe to put up warning cones and to remove the debris. Once the vehicles are past the danger zone, the highway patrolman leaves the highway and the vehicles return to their normal speed.

System Structures

This formal power of systems over individual well-being is huge. Embedding ethical standards into the formal processes within systems and institutions is, therefore, a mandate requiring deliberate collective action within the system. Leaders, individuals, groups, and the collective must have recourse within a system to instill the collective values and ethics into the systems and process and contribute corrections to the rules and norms of the formal system.

Recall that Rawls highlighted the importance of instilling a moral compass into systems, such as institutions, because institutions do not have consciousness nor the ability to hold moral conscience. We have an ethical mandate to develop safeguards to protect liberty for those we love and lead by working to develop collective efficacy and individual autonomy within the systems where we live, work, worship, and learn.

Caveat: When being together with others causes damage and results in regressive learning, or reduces one's power to improve the situation, the group is not healthy and the social contracts, rules, and norms need to be corrected, or the relationships ended.

Formal Structures

The LOVS framework emphasizes structuring the formal system within an organization in ways that

- support development of individual skills,
- provide opportunities for collaborative planning,
- identify and deliver professional development, and
- share leadership where appropriate (Hanson, Bangert, and Ruff, 2016).

Informal Structures

Open vital systems promote feelings of purpose within members by providing opportunities for social contribution, (giving of oneself for the benefit of others). When individuals perceive vital leadership promoting safety, open communication, and giving support when needed, the result is sharing of knowledge and creation of shared meaning.

When formal systems and VL support the development of skills of the members to perform their jobs and to self-regulate (to do no harm to others) in the social context, then the systems, laws, and hierarchies in the formal structure increase in flexibility. Increased flexibility provides more power to the individuals in their locus of control, and they are able to respond to challenges more readily. (Recall the analogy of the birds flocking together.)

Informal system structures develop open communication and support outside of the formal job descriptions and meet the relational needs of the members. The types of relationships built are positive, trusting, broad-reaching, and inclusive. The LOVS informal system exists within the formal structures and continues outside the walls of the organization. Organizational citizenship behaviors are included and compare favorably with those described in a growth mindset culture (Hanson, 2015; Niqab et al., in process).

Example of Open Vital System

Wikipedia is one example of von Bertalanffy's description of a healthy open system demonstrating flexibility in processes and vitality for both the individuals and the organization. The vision driving Wikipedia is to provide "a world in which every single person on the planet is given free access to the sum of all human knowledge" (Wales, 2006, para. 1).

The Wikipedia organization is managed by volunteers, and as its founder, Jimmy Wales, explained, "[W]e're very flexible about the social methodology, because ultimately, the passion of the community is for the quality of the work, not necessarily for the process that we use to generate it" (17:45).

Key points to remember

- Three primary elements are described that human motivation: autonomy, mastery, and purpose.
- There is a difference between sense making and decision making.
- A primary purpose of a healthy human social organization is the creation of common meaning together that will generate a greater benefit to the individuals and group.
- Vital leadership, formal systems, and informal systems are three elements that interact to contribute to the creation of healthy organizations described as leadership within open vital systems (LOVS).
- Healthy organizing requires individual identity, social identity, and transcendent self-awareness.

Chapter 11

Keeping Healthy by Being Open to Feedback

The biggest obstacle to discovery . . . is the illusion of knowledge.

—Daniel J. Boorstin, in Krucoff (1984, p. K8)

Those who cannot change their minds cannot change anything.

—George Bernard Shaw

The ability to receive and use feedback is an indicator of emotional well-being. Individuals who are emotionally healthy trust others and develop strong relationships. Healthy interpersonal relationships are key to developing an accurate worldview, correcting errors in prior learning, and building common understandings with whom we work and live. For example, The Institute for Education and Transformation explained school improvements occur through developing positive relationships between teachers (Poplin and Weeres, 1992).

One's mindset is built from the results of one's internal cognitions and feelings and feedback from social interactions (Bandura, 1988). Individuals use feedback to make and test predictions. They create mental maps of their world to decide how to take action. Feedback loops help individuals develop healthy values through modeling and learning through instruction. The feedback loop can also include self-reflection and reflection on transcendent referents, both critical components to developing higher cognitive skills.

In contrast, if we develop an overreliance on our own thinking, the result is a one-sided, self-centered worldview. When we close ourselves off from others, we limit the input available to develop healthy skills to act in our world. Painful experiences often result in negative feelings. As previously discussed, regressive learning may result if the individual lacks sufficient social support to create positive meaning and develop a positive self-image.

The individual may create an internal cycle of withdrawal and closing off from others. Withdrawal behaviors often serve a healthy protective purpose in an abusive or adverse setting. Regressive learning may result in patterns of withdrawal that will limit one's ability to grow, learn, and improve one's life experience. Habitually abusive or adverse situations, or environments, need to be corrected before an individual with a closed-off feedback loop can develop trust.

Often professional help is needed to mentor and advise an individual with regressive learning to healthy functioning. Recall the discussion in the section on overcoming regressive learning.

Caveat: Being closed to feedback can also occur in systems and institutions in a society. As in the Milgram (1974) experiments and many real-world situations, individuals can become agents, acting in behalf of a system toward goals that do not align with their own values.

THE FEEDBACK LOOP

The following section and figures 11.1–11.3a provide a description of how different types of communication in feedback loops contribute to our ability to grow and learn.

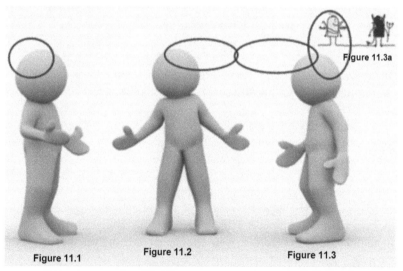

Figure 11.1   Figure 11.2   Figure 11.3

Figures 11.1–11.3a.   Model of feedback loops used in communication. *Source*: © 3D People Talking © Nasir1164 | Dreamstime.com File ID: 23867836 and Devil and Angel © N.I | Dreamstime.com File ID: 11722479.

Figures 11.1–11.3a show a model of individual communication using feedback loops.

Figure 11.1 (*closed-off feedback loop*) is a model of a person with a self-oriented feedback loop. The person represented in figure 11.1 will experience reduced functioning because he or she is unwilling, or unable, to receive feedback from others and is not open to contribute. This limits new skill creation and results in fewer choices and lowered flexibility.

This individual represents someone who may have experienced difficult and painful relationships, an organic or physical limitation such as sensory impairment, or information processing issues.

Figure 11.2 (*sharing ideas and receiving feedback*). The person represented in Figure 11.2 is a model of one communicating ideas and thoughts and receiving feedback from another person. The ability to receive constructive feedback provides data to help correct errors in one's internal mental models. Over time, one uses this feedback to continually re-shape one's personal and social identities.

When one has healthy relationships and receives useful feedback, one can create new information and knowledge to be used for new skill sets. Ultimately, positive constructive feedback can contribute to one's willingness to stay engaged and will result in increased power of personal choice leading to improved functioning and well-being.

Figure 11.3 (*well-balanced feedback loop and transcendent reflection*). The person represented in figure 11.3 represents an individual with a well-balanced feedback loop. This person models openness to receive communication from others. The person in figure 11.3 also uses a transcendent moral referent as a point for reflection, represented in figure 11.3a. Self-reflection and transcendent reflection are used to challenge one's beliefs, to correct and improve one's thoughts and memories, and to internalize transcendent values. This process is part of transformative learning.

When individuals can rely on the feedback they receive from others, they are supported in the process of correcting misguided thinking and mistaken ideas. Useful feedback helps in identifying personal and system biases. Individuals open to learn use feedback to build new, increasingly accurate knowledge that helps them improve and grow. Trust is built as one experiences consistent meaningful and reliable feedback from peers and leaders.

Recall that *trust* is our belief that others in the group will provide a benefit to us and do us no harm. Trust supports a cohesive integration of activities, enables cooperation, and provides perceptions of stability (Reed, Vidaver-Cohen, and Colwell, 2011). Trust is a necessary antecedent of collective efficacy, which subsequently improves group functioning (Tarter and Hoy, 2004).

Leaders can develop healthy feedback loops in their organization by ensuring the individuals' and collective's values are reflected in the decisions, plans, goals, strategies, and actions of the organization.

Systems and structures that promote effective feedback include the following elements:

- Teaching skills to work together and how to give and receive healthy feedback
- Opportunities for practicing new skills in context
- Trained facilitators providing social support for emotional self-regulation
- Facilitating challenging dialogues for reflection
- Providing time for individuals to work and plan together
- Promoting a balance between individual identities and social identity in the group (Hanson, 2015)

MINDSET AND FEEDBACK LOOPS

One is constantly re-making one's beliefs by comparing feedback and input from one's environment with one's prior memory. Figure 11.4 shows how the feedback loop fits into the previous model of goal alignment for well-being and happiness. Notice how when the feedback is positive the individual stays in the loop toward goal attainment and a growth mindset. When feedback is negative, a shift to a fixed mindset may occur, and feelings of helplessness leading to withdrawal can result (Herrmann and Brandstätter, 2015).

THE INFLUENCE OF THE GROUP

The group can provide a sense of belonging and cohesiveness that supports individuals in crisis situations. The power of the group is used in behavioral change models, such as in overcoming prior regressive learning (Nardi, Wozner, and Margalit, 1986). For example, consider a student who avoids taking courses requiring math proficiency because he or she had performed poorly in math courses as a child. However, the student has a goal to become an engineer.

To overcome the student's prior negative memories, the school counselor encourages the student to sign up for individual tutoring and to participate in study groups. The positive relational support the student receives and the

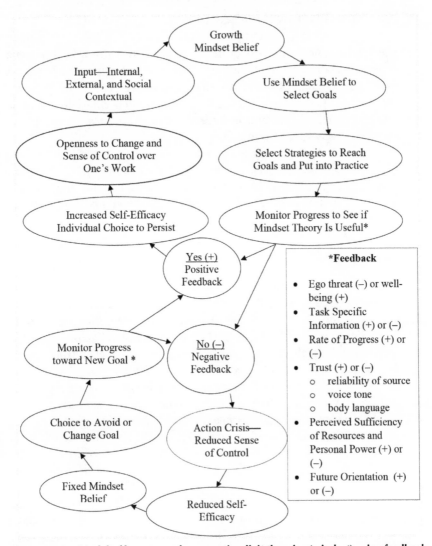

Figure 11.4. Model of how we make up our implicit theories (mindset) using feedback.

explicit description of specific tasks needed for improvement helps him or her become more proficient at math. The student reframes his or her perceptions of himself or herself as experiences of success increase.

A shift to a belief in the ability to grow and learn through one's own effort leads to a growth mindset. The new mindset supports the student to eventually take the math courses for his or her major.

MONITORING PROGRESS TOWARD GOALS

Self-management, or the process of monitoring progress toward one's goals, begins automatically once one chooses to engage and work toward a goal. Feedback is a large part of the monitoring process that occurs internally and in a social context. Feedback is used in developing individual motivations, feelings, and beliefs. Projection and reevaluation are critical elements that occur along the way to determine if one will persist.

If the feedback one receives is poor or if one does not see progress at a timely rate toward one's goals, one may lose a sense of control, shift to a fixed mindset, and emotionally or physically withdraw. An individual may also decide the context or group goals are not aligned with his or her personal goals, lose commitment, and withdraw.

Goal Avoidance

Avoidance behaviors can be intrinsic (personally motivated) or extrinsic (outwardly motivated). For example, students entering high school often express feelings that if they have to try hard to learn something, they must not be smart. In order to protect self-image, when students fail to receive the necessary type, quantity, quality, and timeliness of feedback to meet intrinsic goals, they may shift their focus to a fixed mindset and withdraw.

Their new goals will be less challenging or they may stop trying if the work seems difficult. When an individual has a fixed mindset, even if the structure of the classroom provides quality materials and instruction, a student may withdraw from challenging one's own thinking at the risk of revealing one's errors and making mistakes. Instead, the student may choose to meet the extrinsic expectations of the teacher or parent and focus just on outcomes such as grades.

If the student still fails to achieve the grades desired, he or she may make up an excuse, "I didn't really try because I didn't want to do it." An excuse made to explain one's prior behavior is called a post hoc attribution, making stories that explain one's behavior after the fact. We all do it.

A positive feedback loop can contribute to students' perception of the potential for successful outcomes. For example, teachers, managers, parents, and leaders can make sure to provide information and time to practice mastery strategies, psychosocial supports, resources, and a belief others can grow and learn. This can help overcome fixed mindsets. The process requires effort, which is necessary for everyone to learn and grow (Hanson, 2017a).

Influence from the College Context on Goal Pursuit

Researchers studied the influence of the college context on students with STEM majors and found the students shifted to a fixed mindset when they received negative feedback about their progress before changing their major or dropping out of college. Schools and organizations can develop systems that support individuals to seek help. Organizational supports include developing systems and processes that provide open feedback loops to ensure students are able and willing to persist through challenges (Dai and Cromley, 2014; Kang, Scharmann, and Noh, 2004; Thornton and McEntee, 1995; Tourangeau, Rasinski, Bradburn, and D'andrade, 1989).

Key points to remember

- Healthy interpersonal relationships are key to developing an accurate worldview, correcting errors in prior learning, and building common understandings with whom we work and live.
- One's mindset is built from the results of social interactions and the feedback one receives.
- Feedback loops help individuals develop healthy values through modeling and learning through instruction.
- If the feedback one receives is poor, and if one does not see progress at a timely rate toward one's goals, one may lose a sense of control and shift to a fixed mindset.
- A leader can develop healthy feedback loops in his or her organization or group by teaching skills for giving and receiving healthy productive feedback and providing time in the day for individuals to work in teams and collaborate to solve problems together.

Chapter 12

Developing Your Connections

No man is an island, entire of itself. . . . Any man's death diminishes me, because I am involved in mankind; and therefore never send to know for whom the bell tolls; it tolls for thee.

—Donne, *Meditation 17: Devotions upon Emergent Occasions*

At the heart of all organizing is relationship building. MacIver (1949) described the highest form of life as the most social. *Social* refers to the ability to form positive relationships. Relationships take a variety of forms. This chapter describes ways individuals form connections and how they are used to create learning on three levels: individual, team, and organizational.

Though organizations aren't actually entities, an organization can learn by developing the collective memories of the individuals in them. Individuals can improve through productive learning. Individual learning does not necessarily transfer to the organizational level. The saying that to improve an organization, you must improve the individuals in them is only part of the story. Transferring individual learning into the organization requires not only high individual skills but also relationship building and relational learning (Courtney, Navarro, and O'Hare, 2007).

A sense of connection to others is the result of being acknowledged and feeling valued for how you see yourself, for how others see you, and for your contribution in the group. In addition to this, routines and rituals that are repeated over time build a subconscious feeling of connection. The long-term employees, or group members, become the storehouse of an organization's *stories*.

An organization's stories reflect the shared norms, values, and history of the group and develop connection between its members. New members learn to identify with the group through images displayed (school or company logos and mottos), participation in rituals (team sports, afternoon gatherings), spending time together listening to the stories, in formal training, in collaborative problem solving, planning, shared decision and sense making.

Vital leaders can find important strategies in the concept of growth mindset that will support building strong connections between those they love and lead.

BONDING VERSUS BRIDGING

Two significant types of relationships have been identified between individuals in a social context known as *bonding* and *bridging*. The concepts of bonding and bridging give us a way to talk about how individuals relate to one another (Geys and Murdoch, 2010). Bridging, bonding, team activities, and goal alignment all work together to develop the ability of individuals to learn individually and collectively resulting in organizational learning and growth.

Bonding

Bonding can be described as heartfelt relationships, and occurs between individuals when they see each other as similar. The building of bonding relationships between group members facilitates the development of social capital (relationship power). Bonding also results in automatic forgiveness of small errors and omissions. Mutual trust develops when demonstrating a willingness to conform to group norms, leading to the maintenance of a positive status quo (Carlin and Love, 2013).

When groups come together as part of a system, or institution, such as a school or workplace, individuals are often quite diverse in their backgrounds, beliefs, and behaviors. Leaders, with vital awareness, have a way of seeing beyond the differences of the individuals and finding common collective goals that align with diverse individual goals. This leads to the development of trust, bonding, and collective efficacy in a group resulting in a healthy social organization.

Where bonding does not occur between individuals in the group, it is usually because of significant differences between the individual self-identities. A lack of safety in the group context, unhealthy communications, or informal hierarchies that interrupt the development and implementation of healthy processes can also contribute. Illegitimate goals of informal hierarchies are common and disrupt the development of collective efficacy as they seek to advance personal agendas that differ from the group's stated goals. You may refer to the section on *politics* for a review of this concept.

Bridging

Bridging relationships can be developed when the individuals have little in common, or are operating under market norms, by finding something to work toward that provides a mutual benefit to the members of the group (Fisher,

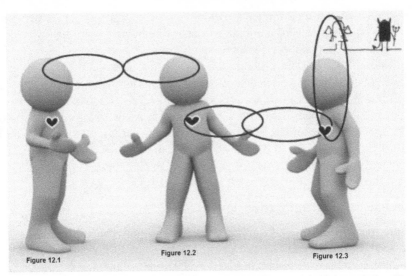

Figure 12.1   Figure 12.2   Figure 12.3

Figures 12.1–12.3.   Model of feedback loops for bonding and bridging relationships. Source: © **3D People Talking** © **Nasir1164 | Dreamstime.com File ID: 23867836 and Devil and Angel** © **N.l | Dreamstime.com File ID: 11722479.**

Ury, and Patton, 2011; Kahneman, 2011). Figures 12.1–12.3 show how bonding and bridging relationships have different feedback loops.

The individuals represented by figures 12.1 and 12.2 are a model of a bridging relationship under market norms. Figures 12.2 and 12.3 show a model of individuals experiencing bonding behavior under conditions of social norms. Figure 12.3 also shows an individual exercising a transcendent moral referent for reflection such as would be demonstrated by behaviors of a leader with vital awareness working to develop open vital system structures.

HEALTHY CONNECTIONS

When people collect together, they usually have a variety of reasons for coming; a primary reason being self-preservation. Recall that participating in collective action does not mean giving all of oneself to the group. One must identify explicit reasons why individuals have assembled for collective action (the values that motivate their behavior) and then identify the relevant goals within that context.

Building healthy relationships through appropriate styles of connecting can facilitate shared sense making, leading to improved organizational and individual outcomes. Discernment is required in order to determine when to bond and when to bridge. Bonding occurs through connecting with the heart in safe emotional environments. Bridging can be efficient and effective to obtain consensus toward a common goal, while being aware that individual commitments may not follow safe social norms.

Caveat: Bonding and bridging are choices one makes about the style of one's connections. When people demonstrate unsafe behaviors, it is important to withdraw and to protect oneself on all levels. Reconnect only when you have determined that those with whom you are working or living have established safe behaviors and follow processes that are just and fair. Individual resilience is the ability to understand how to use discernment in the level and style of connection one makes to maintain one's well-being.

Leadership and Connection

Figure 12.4 shows a model of the difference between individual activity with un-contextualized and unaligned goals within a system versus a healthy system with contextualized and aligned values and goals. Vital leaders contribute in two ways to the development of open vital systems:

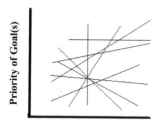

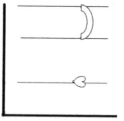

Uncontextualized Goals   **Contextualized Goals**

Goals may change over time and context when they are not aligned. Individuals bring personal and competing goals to the workplace, or group, when explicit efforts have not been made to agree on specific, legitimate goals for the group.

Aligned goals are explicitly stated and agreed upon and remain as priorities when they are contextualized.

– The bottom line represents bonding relationships (values match)

– The top two lines are bridging relationships (values differ but mutual benefits are found in working toward aligned goals)

Figure 12.4.   Model of un-contextualized and unaligned values and goals in a system versus contextualized aligned values and goals in an organization.

through transformational leadership to support identification of legitimate goals in the system that align with the individuals' personal goals (contextualized) for a healthy organization (social-relational norms) and through managerial leadership that provides resources and support for the growth of individuals and system structures that support relational learning.

Market norms will prevail (equitable exchange) in systems that do not recognize and align individual goals (e.g., personal development and safety) with system goals. Individuals may come to work for a paycheck though commitment to the organization may be low. Social relationships may form between isolated individuals in the group to meet their personal needs and goals.

LEVELS OF ORGANIZATIONAL LEARNING

Organizational learning can be described as occurring at three levels and has different *types* of learning at each level:

- Individual—involves routine tasks and is resistant to change
- Team—involves nonroutine problem solving with opportunities for action
- Organizational—involves complex solutions by the collective through changing the external environment (Yeo, 2005, p. 379)

Table 12.1 provides types of learning that occur at different levels of organizing.

Table 12.1. Levels of learning in a learning organization and their features

Stages of learning	Level I	Level II	Level III
Senge's disciplines	Individual mental models and personal mastery learning	Team learning changes how people think. The focus is on the manager	Systems thinking develops a shared vision and creates culture (a way of life)
Open systems	Individual control over one's environment, individual's belief in the group's ability to support learning	Collegial teams with open communication working together in the context	System changes that include group decision making and changes in the culture; modeled and supported by the leader

(Continued)

Table 12.1.   (Continued)

Stages of learning	Level I	Level II	Level III
School mindset culture	Individual belief in the faculty's ability to help all students grow and learn	Team collaborations with open communication and support for all	System changes occur through shared leadership, common goals, and a school-wide plan to get there
Academic mindset in the classroom	Develops self-efficacy and individual growth mindset through mastery strategies	Develops sense of belonging through participation in teams	Promotes a sense of task relevance from aligning classroom tasks with individual goals

Source: **Modified from Hanson (2017a), Table 1. Influences on the types of learning from three levels of organizing described in Senge's (2000), Five Disciplines (p. 70).**

Individual Level

People come to organizations with self-images already developed from their homes and social networks. We all have a shared desire to develop and maintain a positive self-image. We want to feel competent and valued for our contributions. Often individuals avoid challenges that could result in failure.

Individuals are most open to new learning during the first few years in a new context. Openness to change begins to decline when in the same context over time because of the natural progression toward establishing routine behaviors. Long-term employees share informal and formal organizational norms with new employees.

Team Level

Team learning promotes an openness to changing how one thinks about things. Assigning team roles that are aligned with the strengths of each individual increases a sense of social contribution and belonging. Individuals choose to develop social identities with their team when they experience recognition and increased personal power from positive responses to their contributions. As trust develops, a bond may develop.

If individuals are too diverse for bonding, the leader can facilitate bridging by developing open communication skills between the individual members and finding mutual benefits of working together (Fisher, Ury, and Patton, 2011). Team learning occurs through collaborative contribution to the organization. Teams contribute to the organizational-level objectives by solving non-routine problems, such as scheduling, project planning, and collaborating on goals.

Organization Level

As teams receive empowerment for action and positive feedback for their contributions to the organization, new organizational role identities develop. Members begin to act differently by conforming to the new understandings resulting in new norms in the organization. Healthy organizational environments produce relational learning when processes and procedures in place provide the following:

- Just practices
- Affirmation of the individuals' identities
- Time in the day for individuals to work together in teams
- Focused professional development for successful teaming
- Workplace skill development
- Aligning personal strengths and goals with organizational goals
- Transformational leadership that supports decentered power distribution
- Support for a balance between individual autonomy and social integration (Courtney, Navarro, and O'Hare, 2007).

Figure 12.5 puts it all together to show how individuals, teams, and the organization develop healthy group identities and roles through bonding and bridging relationships.

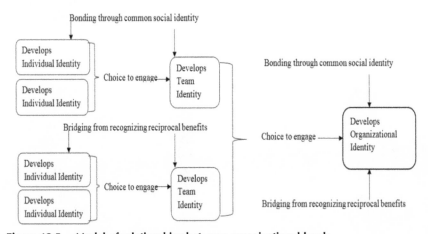

Figure 12.5.   Model of relationships between organizational levels.

MINDSET AND ORGANIZING

Success or failure can be measured by one's willingness to grow and learn within a social context, not only by productivity outcomes. Developing an awareness of how individuals learn and grow at different levels can help vital leaders build open vital system processes. Individual and group efficacy increases when the group creates meaning or participates in collaborative sense making. Where these processes occur, the organization is said to have a growth mindset culture (Hanson, 2015; Hanson, Bangert, and Ruff, 2016).

Key points to remember

- Organizations learn by the individuals building relationships and transferring the individual intellectual capital to the organization.
- The concepts of bonding and bridging relationships give us a way to talk about how individuals relate to one another in the group.
- A sense of connection to others is the result of being acknowledged and feeling valued for how one sees oneself, for how others see him or her, and for one's contribution in the group.
- Organizational learning occurs in three stages: individual, team, and organizational.
- A growth mindset at the organizational level is demonstrated in the culture when the individual members believe all members are able to work together to support all individuals learn and grow.

Chapter 13

Language in Communication

"We have a lot of words like that," Tavi said. "They can mean more than one thing."

"That is stupid," Kitai said. "It is difficult enough to communicate without making it more complicated with words that mean more than one thing."

—Jim Butcher, *Academ's Fury*

Language is a tool to build understanding between people. When used productively, our words can help us to act well together. However, "when a word has multiple meanings, especially if those meanings are implicit, and one move[s] from one [meaning] to another without noticing . . . properties of one meaning might be attributed wrongly to another" confounding our communications (Jozefowiez, 2014, p. 528).

One's mindset can be expressed through the vague concepts of language. Carol Dweck initially named the concept of individual mindset, *individual personality theories,* because she recognized that one's mindset is just a proposition, or idea, about the nature of one's world (Dweck, Chiu, and Hong, 1995). A growth mindset allows an individual to be open to improve the way one communicates by seeking embedded assumptions in the language one uses.

Developing accurate shared meaning can free us from cycles of misunderstanding. The communication we have with others can have both positive and negative influences on our mindset. Recall how one's mindset is used to help explain, predict, and control one's world. Our experiences are stored using language labels mapped onto the brain, so we can retrieve ideas from memory, similar to creating labels for file folders. We use assumptions and feelings when we create meanings of our experiences and these are reflected in the labels we give. When we speak, we include these assumptions within our statements and this can have positive and negative effects on our ability to communicate clearly with others.

For example, we use our assumptions in a process called *attribution* when we make judgments about ourselves and other's behaviors and motives. We use our experiences from the environment, culture, emotions, motivations, and values to make attributions every day. We are mostly successful in this process. We want our communication to be as accurate as possible so we can be even more successful in meeting our goals for love, happiness, safety, fun, and social contribution.

We can increase the accuracy of our attributions by testing our communication skills to identify where errors occur. Isaac Asimov (2017) is quoted as saying, "Your assumptions are your windows on the world. Scrub them off every once in a while, or the light won't come in" (para. 1). When we understand the limitations of language, we can learn to use mental logic principles and self-reflection to observe our thinking processes and "dust off our assumptions."

With self-reflection and an openness to challenge underlying assumptions, we increase our potential for growth. One can learn to manage one's mindset by learning how to minimize errors in communications and build successful relationships that include strong networks, trust, and shared learning to move along the path toward one's goals.

ORGANIZATIONAL COMMUNICATION

Many researchers have shown that biases and incorrect mental constructs result when individuals do not engage in self-reflection and where the organization has not developed a collaborative network between individuals or healthy feedback loops. Peter Senge (1990), a systems scientist and senior professor at MIT, identified several key disciplines supporting the development of organizational learning.

The five disciplines are personal mastery, developing mental models, creating a shared vision, team learning, and systems thinking.

Fundamental Attribution Error

The next sections will give you tools to check the accuracy of your learning, your memories, and processes you use to make attributions. A discussion of attributions will include information on what influences one's motives and ultimately one's behaviors. Recall that *attribution* means to assign a judgment to the motivation for self or others' actions and feelings.

The stories we tell ourselves and others often don't rely on patterns, rules, or evidence from reality. Often, our feelings are used as the basis for how we explain our experiences and those of others we see; that is, we make up stories after the fact based on our current feelings to explain what we experienced (Williams and Ivey, 2001, p. 80).

It is important to make accurate attributions because the judgments we make set a *precedent* for our future actions. The precedents in turn influence our mindset, which determines the choices of goals we select and the strategies we choose to reach them. A biased decision-making process is subject to the fundamental attribution error (FAE) and can result in considering others as "bad actors" (Eisenberg, 2006, p. 1699).

Often we judge others' motives by labeling their *traits,* without considering the influence of the social and physical contexts (Krull et al., 1999; Malle, 2011). For example, recall the example of the video clip of a man running up to another man in an alley and grabbing and pushing him? Did your attribution of the man's motives change after expanding the lens on the situation so you could see the bricks falling off a scaffold (Vucinic, 2005)?

People raised in Western cultures have been shown to automatically resort to spontaneous trait inference; that is Westerners often make attributions based on a *belief* about someone's *traits* (Choi, Nisbett, and Norenzayan, 1999). "Despite having traits, individuals act out of character from their traits most of the time . . . [M]uch of this variation is due to external situations requiring them to change the way they act" (Fleeson and Wilt, 2010, p. 1353–1354).

ABSTRACT LANGUAGE CONCEPTS

Communication becomes increasingly difficult when we move from using language that is concrete to words that are increasingly abstract. For example, an easy statement to understand is, "The cat sat on the mat." Both *cat* and *mat* are concrete objects. Most people can use their senses to test if there is a common understanding of the objects represented by the words and the act of the cat sitting on the mat.

However, what if you said, "The class hates math!" The words in this sentence are abstract ideas. There is a good chance the listener may have difficulty understanding exactly what the speaker means to say. You can improve your communication with others simply by gaining an appreciation for the complexity that occurs when using words for abstract ideas.

Sorites Paradox

The vagueness of language can also create errors in logic that lead to serious problems for individuals making decisions and in relationships with others. How exactly do abstract concepts create problems? The following example called the *sorites paradox* attempts to help us understand.

Consider a heap of sand poured onto a table. The heap consists of individual grains of sand. However, if you remove one grain of sand from the heap at a time, at what point is the heap of sand no longer a heap? Is it still a heap with 40 grains, 20, and so on? The problem with abstract concepts is that they are so vague that the words become unusable to help us distinguish what is actually happening or what it is we are trying to communicate.

Now take the example of the word *organization*. What constitutes an organization? Recall the concept of the organization is actually an abstract language term that refers not to a concrete object but to a *relationship* between individuals (Burns, 1991). Organizations come into existence when individuals agree on, and perform, common expectations for behavior when they are together in a group.

Bandura (2002) warned against the dangers of using abstract ideas as actual entities when he wrote, "There is no emergent entity that operates independently of the beliefs and actions of the individuals who make up a social system" (p. 271). Organizations are created in the minds of the individuals, who participate in them. In the processes of developing ways to communicate, the sorites paradox can explain how labels given to abstract constructs create serious logic errors.

MacIver (1917), professor of sociology, described the concept of a social group this way

> There is no "sum of individuals," no "sum of the parts" of a community. The social relationships of every individual are not outside him. . . . Understand individuals as concrete beings . . . that these *are* society . . . and the metaphysical confusion which leads you to look for something beyond this, something beyond the unsummable social individuals, passes away. (p. 88)

Abstract Idea of the Collective

Abstract constructs create logic errors in thinking because labeling an idea creates a false sense of "entity." As MacIver and Bandura warned, there is a danger that the abstract idea of a concrete *group entity* may take precedence over the actual individuals in the group. As previously discussed, social scientists have debated what constitutes a "society" and the meaning of the concept of a collective.

The distinction between a collection (unorganized) and a collective of individuals is that the collective develops a *collective consciousness* and *social identity*, such as the one suggested in the native term, *Anishinabe,* "Original People." Another example is in the Constitution (1789), "We the People of the United States, in Order to form a more perfect Union."

Social identifications and common norms develop through shared understandings developed over time by interacting together, from the levels of family, community, and upward. Vital leaders must embody the transcendent values of the collective that motivate, uplift, and unite the individuals to act together toward the common goals, for example, "freedom and justice for all."

Through the use of agency and autonomy individuals support the *values of the cause*, not the abstract word used to label the construct. MacIver (1932) in Bierstedt (1981) explained

> For he finds *himself* in the common cause, in the exercise of his individuality through devotion to his family or community or nation or political party or business or trade-union or cultural group. . . . The deeper loyalty, therefore, is not that which slavishly follows the social code – "My country, right or wrong" – but that which responds to it in the spirit and the obligation of the common cause for which it, however imperfectly, stands. (p. 268)

CONSEQUENCES OF LOGIC ERRORS

Abstractions

When we think of an abstract construct of a "group" as a physical entity, rather than as the relationships and memories of interactions between individuals, we can erroneously attribute causality to a nonexistent entity, thereby displacing true responsibility for the actions performed by the individuals in the group. For example, abstract ideas, such as corporations, have been given legal status and have many of the same rights as individuals.

Entities are systems, processes, and hierarchical authority structures, not concrete beings with a will and ability to act. The corporations produce results and carry on business through the actions of individuals. The use of laws to give a legal status, as concrete entities, to words representing abstract ideas imposes changes in our perceptions. Individuals are obliged to behave as if the abstract ideas are fixed and concrete (Freitas, Gollwitzer, and Trope, 2004).

Logic errors such as those described can create a false sense that there exists a collective agreement when a legal entity is created that may not exist between the individuals who work or participate in the system. The result has a significant effect on how we act together in society.

Recall how Milgram demonstrated that amoral authority in the context of a system can influence individuals to perform behaviors to which they are morally opposed?

The manipulation of language can give some individuals tremendous power over others. However, with a conscious awareness of the limitations in the use of language, we can protect ourselves from errors in our logic and improve our individual and collective sense making. We can change and improve how we organize by using logic principles to reflect on whether ethical standards for expected behaviors are embedded and performed in our organizations, schools, communities, corporations, and government processes.

Assumptions

The human mind is influenced by more than language errors. Modeling of cultural norms also influences our judgments and can create serious logic errors embedded in our mental assumptions. The use of false or inaccurate assumptions can create *mental illusions* that can result in fixed mindsets about ourselves and others' behaviors and potentials. For example, in Western cultures there is a bias that most people have the power of independent action.

As a result of our biases, we often make assumptions that people do things because they personally choose to do them and we overlook, or are unaware of, the influences of the social context on one's behavior. When we attribute full power of responsibility to individuals, this prevents us from focusing also on the systems and acting to correct the system pressures that naturally exert themselves on individuals as previously described.

Recall the Milgram (1974) experiment. Most participants were unable to act apart from the directions they were given by the experimenter because of the role they performed. A part of managing one's mindset to maximize one's power of personal choice is recognizing that one's judgments are often influenced by one's culture, context, and inaccurate or incomplete mental representations; and aligning oneself with positive role models.

In order to protect against biases in our assumptions, remember to develop a routine time-off to self-reflect and to challenge your assumptions and beliefs. Also, consider how the design of systems exerts influence on your behaviors. Are there structures in place that prevent you from performing in accordance with your values? How can you work with others to bring transcendent values into system processes for the benefit of all?

USING THE PROCESSES OF SCIENTIFIC INQUIRY

Science is a process that provides a researcher with a framework to explore the world in ways that are meant to collect reliable data from which to make valid conclusions, to make meaning, and to accurately predict and control the world around us (Tyson, 2015). The framework of science was developed to be a window on the unseen world and to create a rich understanding that mirrors reality (Drack, n.d., p. 8).

The accuracy of the models created using the scientific method underlies the studies researchers perform. These models are often not a matter of debate because the underlying theories are needed to provide a framework, as a lens, to design the studies and to understand the data collected (von Bertalanffy, 1968, p. 83). This is much the same way an individual's mindset works. You become the researcher.

In order to develop accurate theories, you need to develop the ability to create a growth mindset as a lens through which you view the world. Be sure that you avoid and correct cognitive biases and errors in your thinking along the way. As you begin to understand how the use of language labels can create errors in how we interact with and view our world, you can protect against misunderstandings by avoiding the misuse of abstract language ideas as if they are concrete rather than relationships or processes.

When you watch television, try to identify when media, advertisements, news anchors, or politicians use words to advance market or political agendas. Be cautious to identify biases in things others say. Reflect on your use of words. This will help you ensure your words bring clarity to the conversation and respect the rights and autonomy of others.

The first step in the process of managing your mindset to create more accurate meaning is to develop an underlying awareness and appreciation of the concepts presented in this book. An example of how knowing about these processes can change how you think and act follows.

A manager in a business held a meeting with the department members. When one asked for funds to purchase needed resources, the manager shared that there wasn't a budget line for the purchase. Everyone grumbled about how irrational it seemed to have the money in the budget though not be able to spend it because there was no budget line. The meeting ended with a bad feeling all around.

Later, the manager recalled having recently read of the concept of challenging one's assumptions. He recognized he had developed a negative bias toward the company based upon the assumption that he did not have control over the budget in his department. He had reduced his sense of power of personal choice. Upon reflection, he recognized he had created a blocked communication channel.

The new meaning he created enabled him to act in a positive manner. He went to his supervisor and openly shared the request for materials and the difficulty he felt for not having a budget line for the purchase. The supervisor informed the manager that a process did exist for the type of purchase the manager requested. Another department's budget had a code that covered all purchases of this type.

The manager returned to his department and told the coworker how to process the request and the materials were soon ordered. The manager's feelings changed and his work experience in the company improved. The manager and department members no longer grumbled. The coworkers felt high regard for their manager's wisdom in being willing to admit his assumptions had been inaccurate and for his ability to create a positive work environment for them.

If the manager had not been open to challenge his assumptions, to act in proxy for the team, and to develop improved communication resulting in improved understanding, the department may have continued with disgruntled feelings and the resources would not have arrived on a timely basis to do the job.

Can you think of ways you can challenge your assumptions in areas where you feel blocked or have difficulty communicating with others? What new information can you find to propose complementary solutions to situations and raise the level of belief in the ability of the organization, teams, and individuals to learn and grow together?

TRAIT VERSUS STATE THEORY

Traits are considered to be enduring dispositions, responses to internal and external events that the individual expresses in a variety of contexts consistently over time, for example, fearless, capable, and confident. Reliance on traits for predicting self and others' behaviors can generate a belief in fixedness and a fixed mindset: "I'm not smart." This has been observed occurring in research in Western cultures so often that it has been termed the *fundamental attribution error.*

However, the belief in the potential for self and others to change through learning and effort opens the possibility for growth. The following open communication directed to a helpful other is an example of how to use a growth mindset and power of personal choice to overcome a fixed mindset belief. "I haven't had a lot of success in the past with _____ (Fill in your current challenge area in the blank line.), and I feel threatened by the tasks. I am willing to overcome my feelings even though I have had them for a long time. Will you help me?"

The concept of *traits* can be contrasted with the concept of *states*. How you feel emotionally is termed an *affective state*. States are described as temporary emotional responses to external stimuli, for example, angry, sad, and happy. Your state can influence how you behave. This is referred to as *manifestation.*

When others see your behavior, and if they believe traits are permanent, or fixed, they will attribute the cause of your behavior to a trait and may not consider contextual influences that may have contributed to your behavior

(Job, Bernecker, and Dweck, 2012). The way we use words can create a circular reasoning in our logic that reinforces the social belief in abstract ideas as concrete fixed objects leading to fixed mindsets and inaction.

Both traits and states are abstract concepts people use to describe and explain their world (Chaplain, John, and Goldberg, 1988). As abstract constructs, traits and states are subject to the *sorites paradox* described by the question: "When is a state no longer a state, but becomes a trait?" You can manage your mindset by being careful with the words you use. You can change your beliefs resulting in improvements in your power of personal choice.

Weaknesses of Trait Theory

As previously explained traits are inferred, abstract, language constructs, not real things. Therefore, traits are impermanent and can change based on the context, priming, and motivations of the individual. Often there is a lack of verifiable evidence of the reliability of the attributions one makes when assigning traits to oneself, or others. The measurement of abstract ideas, like *traits*, has come under question by some researchers in part because the feelings and beliefs of the rater affect his or her evaluations of a trait being measured.

This is called rater bias or rater error. In survey research, many scales have been developed for measuring traits as if they are fixed characteristics of a person that determine their behavior. The measurement instruments researchers use often fail to accurately account for the influences from the context in the survey items' construct definitions being rated by the participants.

Washing the Windows

Do you express critical opinions of your family, school, or organization without using self-reflection and inquiry into your own biases and behaviors? Are you caught up in making attribution errors of others' based on inferred traits and motives? Are you inflexible in your behaviors and do you feel challenged in new contexts and situations? Do you make up stories to protect your self-image?

If you answered "yes" to any of these questions, you've increased your chances for success and growth by recognizing areas for growth. You have already come far along the path to establishing new patterns that change the old patterns in your brain, just by reading and reflecting on what you read in this book. Continue routinely to "wash the windows" of your assumptions that lead to biases and inaccuracies in your mental models.

The next sections discuss more about how to improve the processes you use to create your beliefs and develop communication styles with your family, friends, and those with whom you work and live.

Key points to remember

- Language is developed within a sociocultural framework.
- The vagueness of human language, used as a tool for communicating one's ideas, often results in a lack of sense (incoherence).
- This has serious consequences for managing one's mindset, which is the basis for the meanings one assigns to experiences that are used to make our judgments of self and others.
- You can overcome your own errors that become embedded in memories and result in poor judgments and the fundamental attribution error so common in the West.
- Use the process of scientific inquiry to explore possibilities for new ways of thinking that open your communication with others.

Chapter 14

How Culture Affects Your Mindset

A nation's culture resides in the hearts and in the soul of its people.

—Mahatma Gandhi

If we find we are not as successful in our ability to act in our world as we would like, we need look no further than to the processes we use to evaluate and structure the data we receive. *Epistemology* is another word that can be used for describing the processes of developing our worldview. Epistemology is how we evaluate the nature of knowledge, the rationality of our beliefs, and the stories we create to justify our beliefs.

For example, teachers have epistemologies, or mindsets, about teaching and learning that influence their choices of instructional practices and their students' success. Teachers with fixed mindsets are more likely to use behaviorist strategies in their classrooms and have fewer personal relationships with their students (Blackwell, Trzesniewski, and Dweck, 2007; Farrington et al., 2012).

The focus of this chapter will be the study of the processes that we use to develop our mindsets and how this significantly influences how we relate to our world. In order to manage your mindset you need to understand your worldview and the influences exerted on you by your culture of origin. In this chapter you will read about *how* the difference between an Eastern and Western worldview predisposes one to either a fixed or growth mindset.

Worldview is the central structure of how one conceives of reality. One's belief system is influenced by a common agreed-upon view by members of a culture and is the source from which proceeds the value system. A worldview is central to every culture, subconsciously interacting and influencing all aspects of the shared reality of its members (Marsden, 2003, p. 56).

The following quote explains how one's language of origin influences our thinking and experience:

> The structure of ordinary language reflects and in part creates the psychology of the people who use that language, through the embedding of implicit theories in terms of which experience is organized. (Sternberg, 1985b, p. 1111)

Differences in cultural worldviews and values are reflected in the group's behaviors. For example, Eastern cultures tend to reward peace and cohesion of the group more highly than individual expression and independent action. Eastern culture groups also provide more support for individual emotional self-regulation than those in Western cultures (Spector et al., 2001).

Caveat: Researchers study human behavior on several levels, including individual, group, and organizational. Please note that as this discussion progresses, group-level research results are only generalizations and may not apply to every individual in the group under study (Hofstede, 2001; Schwartz, 1992). For example, the values of independence and interdependence can vary between individuals within the group as well as from the group average. Individuals in context-centered cultures, also referred to as collectivist cultures, may act independently, and individuals in individualistic, or person-centered, countries may act collectively.

CONTEXT-CENTERED AND PERSON-CENTERED CULTURES

Our culture of origin deeply influences us and helps to shape our perceptions. For example, North Americans and Europeans more often view themselves as independent, autonomous, unique, and self-contained. Asians, Africans, and Latin Americans are more likely to view their identities as connected to family, friends, and coworkers (Markus and Kitayama, 1991).

Person-Centered Cultures

Person-centered cultures, such as the United States, Canada, and Western European countries, focus on individuals as the center of decision making, suggesting individuals have independence in the choices they make. The focus is on a person's skills and traits rather than on how one relates to the group or to authority. A person-centered focus would be evidenced by a tendency to give priority to a person's skills over his or her fit to the group when selecting for a position.

Individuals in person-centered cultures show less flexibility because they are less likely to take in information from the context for use in decision making.

Context-Centered Cultures

Context-centered cultures focus on understanding relationships. Individuals in context-centered cultures show increased flexibility and the ability to use contextual data in their meaning-making (Choi, Nisbett, and Norenzayan, 1999). In Eastern cultures, such as Japan, Korea, and China, individuals give high consideration to how one fits in with the group rather than to one's traits or skills. This explains why in a context-centered culture, one might consider a person with only good job skills to be untrustworthy.

Easterners place a high value on relational concepts such as indebtedness, connection, familiarity, emotions, and social harmony (Choi, Nisbett, and Norenzayan, 1999). Easterners made fewer errors in research studies when judging the motives of others' behaviors because they recognized the power of influences on the choices of others from their environment, emotions, relationships, and other context variables.

Easterners view asserting one's opinions over promoting harmony as immature. Mature individuals are described as valuing interrelatedness and having a positive self-identity through developing positive relationships with others in the group.

Critical Thinking

In a context-centered culture, critical thinking relates to reflection about *one's own beliefs* and is not an expression of evaluating others. In other words, critical thinking is not critically speaking or judging others' behaviors or qualities. As one matures, critical thinking becomes more about developing positive group identification and healthy social norms than about making attributions and evaluative judgments of others.

Similarly, when individuals give a higher priority to developing collective efficacy (CE), they recognize, acknowledge, and support the needs of the other individuals in the group, seeking harmony rather than highlighting differences. Understanding the influences on one's perceptions and values is important because we use them to make judgments that can create conflict within our groups leading to fixed and resistant mindsets.

Fixed mindsets prevent improvements in one's mental models and limit opportunities for transformative learning. The result may have a negative effect on one's emotions and perceptions. Recall how one's emotional state sets a precedent, or creates the baseline, for our future judgments.

INFLUENCE OF CULTURE ON BEHAVIOR

Evidence shows that the influence of one's cultural context is an important consideration in one's judgments and decision making. The context must be considered when determining how one behaves, because individuals find themselves participating in a variety of groups and systems over the course of their days and lives. Have you noticed you may act differently in one context, or group, than in another?

As previously discussed, a Western mindset is considered individualistic and an Eastern mindset may be considered collectivist. However, depending on the context, the reverse can be demonstrated. Westerners can act collectively and Easterners can be shown to act independently. An example is provided here to explore the importance of this topic for understanding the influence of the context on one's mindset.

As a group, the behaviors of drivers on the roadways in the United States can generally be described as orderly. Generally, people follow the safety regulations that provide structure to keep individuals safe and timely in their travels. In contrast, an individual from a large Eastern country explained that, in the cities of her homeland, the individuals were *less* likely to follow the rules of the road. Travel was less orderly, even challenging or chaotic at times, due to the unpredictable behavior of individuals traveling on the roads.

This is a counterintuitive example of how individuals in a collectivist culture act independently in a specific context (driving), while individuals in the United States, where independence is valued, act collectively (Hofstede, 2001). Researchers found Westerners tended to act collectively with their out-groups, such as with the highway authority and fellow travelers, yet more independently with their in-groups (family, coworkers, and peers).

Easterners were shown to act more independently toward their out-groups and more collectively with their family and work units (Markus and Kitayama, 1991).

The importance of this example is that the descriptors of individualism and collectivism are strongly influenced by the existing context. To avoid errors in judgment, you are encouraged to consider the context when describing or evaluating an individual's or groups' actions. This finding has significant implications for your mindset. Consider ways the context may influence the way you think about others and yourself.

IN-GROUPS AND OUT-GROUPS

An example of Eastern individualistic expression in a collectivist society follows to help develop an understanding of the meaning of in-group and out-group. In 2008, the Chinese hosted the Olympic Games in Beijing. The artist, Guo-Quiang, created amazing pyrotechnic displays with a goal to bring honor to China through his work. However, he was criticized by his artist peer group for working with the government in a more practical application of his art.

The in-group's complaint was that the artist had given up his artistic purpose in order to serve a political goal. Guo-Quiang stated, "It seems I've compromised my work on this time after time. . . . Art needs to be free." However, Zang Yimou, film and artistic director of the Beijing Olympics, explained, "Art needs to be free, but these projects have political requirements. . . . Artists who grew up in free Western countries are not able to understand this" (McDonald, 2016).

The in-group in this context was comprised of the artists who held common norms of artistic purity. The government was considered the out-group by the artists because the government group held values of pragmatism and political and social control. This example highlights how social identities develop through commonly held beliefs among the members creating in-group associations.

In sum, members of both Eastern and Western cultures can express individualistic and collectivist worldviews depending on the context and in reference to a particular group. Can you identify when Guo-Quiang was acting collectively and when he was acting individualistically? More will be shared about the influence and importance of culture and the group norms on one's beliefs and behaviors in future sections.

COMMON CULTURAL NORMS FACILITATE COMMUNICATION

As previously discussed, trust is required for relational learning and contributes to the resilience and adaptability of the organization. Collective efficacy results from building group-level trust and aligning group roles with individual goals. In diverse cultural environments, building CE takes effort and the individuals need high cognitive skills. Good communication takes time to develop, sometimes years of working together.

Long-term relationships contribute to the ability to perform complex tasks in a group setting. An example follows.

In recent years, China has expanded the country's road system and built some of the longest and highest bridges on the planet. The accomplishment has become one of the most ambitious and challenging engineering feats in the world. A project manager overseeing construction of one of the large bridge-building projects was asked how they were able to perform such complex and challenging construction projects and avoid major setbacks.

The manager explained that the workers' ability to effectively communicate with each other was a major contributor to successful operations. On each project the supervisors attempted to hire team members who had grown up together in the same small communities. The workers' long-term relationships were viewed as an asset because the individuals had developed similar worldviews and held common social norms resulting in clear communication.

Commonly understood group expectations for behaviors, and similar worldviews, facilitate decision making, prevent errors in communication, and help workers avoid serious mistakes on projects. Where constant change and turnover of personnel occur, or with rapid influxes of new demographics, a group's understanding of accepted norms is reduced and challenges normative accepted cultural behaviors. Miscommunications can easily develop when common worldviews are lacking.

SOCIAL SUPPORT FOR INDIVIDUAL SELF-REGULATION

Parents, teachers, managers, and leaders can learn skills that can help develop emotional self-regulation and resilience in those they love and lead. Psychosocial skills mean psychological and social skills that strengthen the self-image and improve emotional self-regulation, freeing energy for the mental efforts of learning. In individualistic societies there is less tendency for the social group to provide support for an individual's emotional (affective) regulation. Differences can result between cultures at school levels also. Different cultures have been shown to exist between elementary school and secondary school levels as well.

For example, research showed that teachers in secondary schools used behaviorist strategies, developed fewer relationships with students than at the elementary school level, and lacked awareness of how to develop psychosocial skills in the students. This resulted in more students having difficulties when transferring to secondary level including lowered social skills, withdrawal behaviors, and reduced academic success (Blackwell, Trzesniewski, and Dweck, 2007; Farrington et al., 2012; Hanson, Ruff, and Bangert, 2016).

A behaviorist model of discipline overlooks the cognitive emotional aspects influencing one's power of personal choice. Often individuals are labeled as fully responsible for their actions if they disrupt the group because of unmanaged behaviors and or emotional displays. Providing a "blanket against a cold world" can provide supports to individuals who have not had the privilege of modeling for healthy emotional self-regulation, or who experience emotional triggers from traumatic experiences described as ACEs in a previous section.

DIVERSITY AND MULTI-CULTURALISM

Recall that learning is part of a mental process that develops mental maps on the brain used by the individual to create and affirm his or her sense of self. Learning can be described as the progressive development of one's identity. The question becomes, "[W]hat is part of me versus what is not (yet) part of me? (Akkerman and Bakker, 2011, p. 132). We naturally seek similarities in others based on a variety of factors especially appearance, as this validates our personal identity and creates a bond.

Our tendency is to focus on outward appearance and to highlight differences in those we consider different from us. We create labels that group individuals into abstract categories. The language of one's culture of origin contributes to the creation of in-group and out-groups; resulting in a "concrete" sense of "self" and "the other."

This is a beginning to the process leading to a sense of diversity. Recognizing differences has a survival purpose. The world is not always a safe place. Recall how *discernment* is required to identify when others are not safe and how it is important to disconnect, or create a boundary between you and them, even if temporarily. However, in some cases it can prevent the development of trust and collective efficacy in groups.

Boundaries

Recall the discussion earlier on how the process of learning involves expanding one's boundaries of knowing; exploring what is part of oneself and what is part of the "other." The term *boundary,* within the context of diversity and multiculturalism, is defined next:

> *Boundary*—"a socio-cultural difference leading to discontinuity in action or interaction." (Akkerman and Bakker, 2011, p. 133)

Boundaries exist wherever there is a difference in one's expectations and skills with the new situation (requiring new learning and change in self-identity). Recall the example of cultural boundaries between elementary and secondary school levels that make student transitions more difficult (Hanson, Ruff, and Bangert, 2016).

Boundary Crossing

Logic would suggest that system structures and supports be put in place to promote perceptions of safety, predictability, and mutual benefit leading to trust and an openness to new learning, and improvement in one's ability to cross boundaries. A variety of methods have been suggested to create "bridges" to facilitate communication and the ability for diverse others to work together until new learning can occur that empowers individuals to cross their own boundaries.

Successful interactions can lead to relational learning and new shared meanings where vital leaders provide safe and ethical system structures. Shared identities, new individual and social identities, can emerge. Improving communication between diverse others requires facilitated mentoring by known trusted others, spending time together to develop common understandings, and a willingness to challenge one's assumptions (Hanson, Ruff, and Bangert, 2016.)

Diversity versus Multiculturalism

Movements of individuals between countries and communities create increasingly diverse populations in our organizations and social groups. There is a difference between diversity and multiculturalism.

Diversity refers to the differences found within a group, such as gender, age, socioeconomic status, and race.

Multiculturalism refers to the differences between cultures and is usually used in a global context between countries.

Increasing specialization in the workplace also creates unique skill sets and amplifies differences between individuals and groups. Our perceptions of differences and real differences in background, experiences, and skills challenge the flexibility of individuals in the group due to changing cultural norms and reductions in clear communication. As previously stated, building new shared norms of expected behaviors among diverse group members requires high cognitive skills and time together (King, and Shuford, 1996).

The challenge of working in contexts with diverse others becomes how to create opportunities for diverse individuals to act safely together. A key is to structure the day, and workplace, to provide opportunities for individuals to spend sufficient time together, in productive ways, to develop new learning that results in a social advantage to all involved.

Recommendations to Improve Group Outcomes

Promoting a growth mindset has been show to overcome one's implicit biases, increase cultural responsiveness, and reduce stereotype threats (Blackwell, Trzesniewski, and Dweck, 2007; Farrington et al., 2012). The goal is to develop the trust necessary to achieve mutual goals. Other recommendations to improve group outcomes, where diversity presents a challenge, include

- developing skills to engage in challenging dialogue;
- opportunities for self-reflection;
- referring to transcendent values that recognize the value of others;
- assuming responsibility for one's actions;

- providing positive experiences of acknowledgment, repeated over time, through the use of routines and rituals;
- creating "bridges" to work together in teams, build relationships, and common meaning between people;
- artifacts and images can be used as flexible ways to find and develop shared identities;
- providing trusted representatives acting to support the needs of the individuals in the group (Akkerman and Bakker, 2011; Hanson, Bangert, and Ruff, 2016).

Multicultural Lens

Being able to work through the challenges of multicultural environments requires confidence in one's own cultural identity, while being able to accept others' diverse cultural ways of behaving as legitimate. *A multicultural lens* may be developed through which we view the world by early social experiences with diverse others, conditioning over time, and developing skills with other languages.

Cultural responsiveness does not arise automatically. It takes hard work to develop a change in one's beliefs and acceptance of diverse others. Over time, with humility and explicit instruction in the variety of unique cultural mores, a common understanding between group members can develop (King and Kitchener, 1994). The effort is worthwhile because groups are more resilient and effective when they have developed high social capital, including healthy communication, social norms, and trust (Helliwell, Huang, and Wang, 2014).

It is well to remember when working in a multicultural environment that healthy organizing ensures that all individuals derive a benefit from participating in the group. Results of a healthy organization include:

- developing new common understandings as social norms;
- behaviors that are guided by transcendent moral truths;
- shared meaning making;
- improved well-being of all.

Key points to remember

- One's worldview is influenced by one's social environment as well as the way one evaluates the data received.
- In order to make accurate meaning from the data received, you must ensure you reflect on your own biases.

- One's social group and culture has a large influence on how one views the world.
- Individuals raised in Western cultures have a tendency toward spontaneous trait inference, or assigning labels to abstract concepts and judging ourselves and others' motives as trait-based.
- Individuals in Eastern cultures are less likely than Westerners to make the fundamental attribution error in judgments, because they include more context variables as influencing individual behaviors and consider traits as flexible, rather than enduring in all contexts.
- Boundaries are differences that result an individual withdrawing from interacting with others.
- Boundaries are said to develop when there is a difference between one's expectations and one's skills in a new situation. This growth opportunity requires new learning; and may lead to a change in one's individual or social identities.

Chapter 15

A Growth Mindset for a Healthy Individual

It's never too late to start over. If you weren't happy with yesterday, try something different today. Don't stay stuck. Do better.

—Kerry Petsinger (2016)

In order to promote a growth mindset, one must discipline one's mind, heart, body, and spirit. Self-discipline requires balance in thought and an interconnectedness throughout the self. In Western thought and medicine, we break systems into parts. This is the result of a dualistic worldview. The parts aren't necessarily separate or separable. Parts are just names we give to mental concepts we have created. Integration is necessary to put them back together.

We are said to be in integrity when our stories match the actual experience, and our behavior is in agreement with our thinking. When we use our memory of how we felt after our experiences to justify the stories we make to remember them, they may not always match the actual experience. Often self-protection is a motive.

For example, with regressive learning, the actual experiences we have may be connected with fearful emotions. To avoid the negative feelings, the memory may become fixed or locked away, not open for correction even when one's skills and situation have improved. The following quote highlights this idea. "Over the years, I have come to realize that the greatest trap in our life is not success, popularity, or power, but self-rejection" (Nouwen, 2017, para. 2).

One of the greatest mental exercises you can do to is to reconnect your mind, heart, and feelings (sometimes referred to as "gut" or intuition). When you self-reflect, you are acknowledging the entire self. The same two fundamental requirements for healthy social organizing are required for healthy self-organizing:

- Acknowledge yourself
- Agree with yourself (be in integrity with your mind, heart, and spirit)

Having a common goal with yourself means all the parts are working together. Recall how transformative learning results in resolving internal conflicts and tensions by integrating oneself through a transcendent self-awareness.

A HEALTHY MIND, BODY, AND SOUL

A Healthy Mind

Having healthy thoughts has been shown to contribute to one's ability to effectively function and bond with others. As C. S. Lewis (2002) wrote "Hell is a state of mind—ye never said a truer word. And every state of mind, left to itself, every shutting up of the creature within the dungeon of its own mind—is, in the end, Hell" (para. 1). We all need balance to maintain a healthy mind. A healthy mind also requires discipline.

Balance includes integration of one's self, including mind, body, spirit, and emotions. We can find support for exploring and interpreting the real meaning of our basic emotions by developing habits of self-reflection and heartfelt connections with healthy others. We can promote the development of a healthy mind by being open to receive feedback and to share. Integration comes from transformative learning, which provides the ability to safely hold life's tensions arising from conflicts between one's values and one's experiences.

A Healthy Body

The Hippocrates oath, attributed in philosophy of practice to the Greek physician, considered the father of medicine, acknowledges the use of food in ensuring one's health. "I will apply dietetic measures for the benefit of the sick according to my ability and judgment; I will keep them from harm and injustice" (p. e3). Pick the right foods to meet the needs of a balanced metabolism. Too rich of fuel burns up the engine.

The body is designed for balance. Habitual stress, high caloric intake without physical activity, and toxic exposure strain the body's organs as they work to bring the system back into balance. A healthy body requires self-discipline. Avoid activities such as smoking and exposure to toxic chemicals. Instead, exercise to increase flexibility and strength.

Energy Production Systems

The body balances between two systems for energy production, fast and slow. Slow energy production comes from using insulin in the blood (changed to glucose) for healing, growth, work, and energy storage. The fast system kicks in for a fight or flight response when one is stressed (using glycogen from the muscles). When the fast system kicks in, the slow system temporarily stops (Jensen, Rustad, Kolnes, and Lai, 2011). You can use your muscles to exercise, such as walking, to use up the glycogen and turn on the slow system.

Managing Stress

Researchers are suggesting that just the act of thinking that stress is harmful rather than helpful can increase your chance of dying. In research studies, individuals who thought stress was harmful showed constricted blood vessels at the same time their heart rate went up from the actual stressors. This opposing reaction put added stress on the heart and increased their risk of have a heart attack.

Instead, *thinking of stress as a helpful body response to challenges* can increase your health by keeping blood vessels open and blood flowing to the heart when the demand for oxygen has gone up (McGonigal, 2013, 2:23).

Another finding from the research was that stress releases a hormone called oxytocin. Oxytocin works on the brain to drive us to seek connection and support from others to help us. Reaching out to others is one of the behaviors that develops one's resilience. The cycle becomes reinforcing, because as we reach out to others, or as we help others who are experiencing stress, our bodies release more oxytocin, which increases our healing and promotes more connections (McGonigal, 2013).

Hiking and walking with your family and friends is a great response to stress, because it not only uses the fast energy system, it also increases connection, which reduces stress, speeds healing from the damage caused by stress, and allows your body to return to a balanced metabolism.

What happens when individuals can't find or create positive social connections when they experience stress? The following paragraphs have significant implications for society to ensure everyone has "a blanket from a cold world" through developing systems leading to networks of social support and caring.

Initial studies on the addictive properties of narcotics in the 1960s suggested they were *highly* addictive. However, a researcher in the UK suggested it was the social isolation, austere conditions of the Skinner experimental cages, and psychologically abusive testing procedures that drove rats to self-medicate (Alexander, 2008, 2010; Hari, 2015).

To test his hypothesis, Alexander (2010) created "a large housing colony, 200 times the floor area of a standard laboratory cage. There were 16–20 rats of both sexes in residence, food, balls and wheels for play, and enough space for mating. The results of the experiment appeared to support his hypothesis" (Rat Park, n.d., para. 1).

As Alexander (2010) explained,

> We ran several experiments comparing the drug consumption of rats in Rat Park with rats in solitary confinement in regular laboratory cages. In virtually every experiment, the rats in solitary confinement consumed more drug solution, by every measure we could devise. And not just a little more. A lot more. (para. 11)

Microbiome–Home for Microbes

The digestive systems is a home for microbes. Just as you are part of a larger social system, your body is part of a larger, though microscopic, microbiome system. Friendly bacteria support our immune systems and assist us in maintaining our health. What is a microbiome? It consists of trillions of small cells that help our bodies function.

Researchers suggest there are more of the little critters in and on one's body than there are of one's own cells. The probiotics you eat, such as active yogurt cultures, include some of these microbes. In order to maintain a healthy body, we must take care of our microbes, which includes eating healthy foods to promote the growth of "good bacteria." We either help them help us, or we disable them and hurt ourselves (Lloyd-Price, Abu-Ali, and Huttenhower, 2016).

Microbiomes are shared between individuals. Experiments have shown microbes can influence our ability to connect socially and increase our social identification (Archie and Tung, 2015). Microbes in and on the human body have also been shown in experimental studies to have the ability to think and to make decisions on how to organize and respond to their environment. A healthy diverse microbiome helps us connect internally and externally.

Gut

The intestinal tract has a system of cells that function like brain cells called the enteric nervous system. This "brain" is in communication with our larger brain and other subsystems of our body constantly. What we put into our digestive system and how we treat our body affects the ability of these systems to communicate well (Garagnani et al., 2014; Hadhazy, 2010). Low-calorie, high-nutrient foods, such as colorful vegetables, provide the ingredients for health without overburdening your body. Being in contact with nature provides nutrients as well.

A Healthy Soul

A healthy soul provides a guide for one's behavior. Self-reflection can be used to inquire into one's biases and compare the priorities of one's beliefs and actions with a transcendent standard. One can put oneself in perspective by thinking less often of the self and more of others. This is the quality of humility by which one is able to recognize the influence of our actions on others (Lewis, 2002). Transcendent values can be developed from a belief and trust in the goodwill of a moral entity that transcends one's self.

A metaphor for how the soul can be used as a guide is to consider an airplane flying east. The pilot could fly indefinitely and still be flying east. In contrast, if the plane were heading north, once the plane reaches the North Pole a change in direction occurs and the plane is heading south. The pilot can use a compass as a guide. We need markers along our way to know where we are headed and when to change directions. We may not reach perfection, but it is important to have a guide for our decisions (Appel, 2016).

A Healthy Mind/Heart Connection

The heart has millions of brain cells. The heart can think and understand simple emotions like love, hate, fear, safety, happiness, and sadness; yet serves a different function than the brain (Surel, 2014). The heart seeks connection, not self-protection. However, the heart isn't necessarily pure in intentions. Though the heart is childlike, even children by age two were found to have the ability to lie.

The heart can hold grudges, and feel fear, anger, love and safety. To be in integrity with youself, you must acknowledge your heart's feelings and give yourself care and support. All of the qualities of one's self must be in open communication, disciplined, guided by healthy external standards, and integrated into a *flexible system*. When you are in integrity with your self-system, you can more readily develop and maintain healthy relationship with others.

As previously explained, recent studies of body systems revealed important connections and messaging between the brain, heart, and pneumogastric nerve. The heart is in constant communication with the brain. In fact, the heart sends more messages to the brain than the brain sends to the heart. An individual's ability to self-regulate thoughts, emotions, and behaviors is directly associated with the ability of these systems to communicate and to make effective judgments and sense of one's world (Park and Thayer, 2014).

In his book titled *The Secret of Happiness,* Dr. Henry Cloud (2011) shared a summary of research on well-being, or happiness. Three key behaviors that affect happiness, include feeling gratitude, connection, and giving.

Gratitude

Poet David Whyte (2013) wrote, "Gratitude arises from paying attention, from being awake in the presence of everything that lives within and without us" (para. 1). Reflection is necessary to retrain your mind and learn to see life with a grateful attitude. You can uplift your thoughts and feelings by acknowledging the blessings you have.

Remember earlier how the mind rationalizes the emotions and explains our behaviors after the fact? When we let our mind make up stories to be consistent with negative feelings, we can spiral downward into an all-or-nothing dissatisfaction and a sense of entitlement when we don't get what we want. One can manage one's thoughts by reflecting on positive experiences, finding positive meaning in negative experiences, and maintaining a positive focus.

Reach out for support; use your words to express yourself. Think about your thinking, and exercise your mind to support and acknowledge positive feelings of gratitude in your heart. You do this by being present with those you love and seeing the wonderful things that are in your life right now.

Human Connection

Researchers explained that by developing a connection with the heart, one can increase health, happiness, and well-being. As previously explained, human connection is an incredibly important part of human well-being. Connections require face-to-face time together. The more people you meet and the more often you share time together, the greater the likelihood of finding those with whom you can identify, develop common shared goals, and create healthy relationships.

Overcome the all-or-nothing thinking that comes with disappointments. Continue to connect with healthy others. Manage your feelings when things don't go as you hoped or expected. Keep going. If one social activity doesn't work out, don't give up. Inquire into why you feel the way you do. Seek feedback from healthy others. Determine if your failures are just part of the stages of learning.

You may need to make changes in what you do or think to be more successful at meeting and connecting with people. Research new groups and ask others for help and for ideas. Reach out to someone you admire. Following is an example of one person who learned to develop connection by doing all these things.

Dr. Milton Erikson, an eminent psychologist, gave advice to a woman who was discouraged and had lost motivation in life. When Erikson visited the woman at her home, he noticed she had an interest in growing African violets. He told her to find people to whom she could give her violets. She began to take violets to new mothers in the maternity ward in the hospital, to people in her church celebrating birthdays, and to those celebrating anniversaries.

Dr. Erickson redirected the woman's negativity by focusing her strengths to create positive connections. Her motivation for life returned, and when she died many years later, a newspaper article reported her death with the following headline, "African Violet Lady Mourned by Thousands" (O'Hanlon, 1994).

Giving

Batson and Shaw (1991) explained that people are pro-social, meaning they derive happiness both by being with and by doing things for others (Helliwell, Huang, and Wang, 2014). Giving of ourselves to others is a necessary element of heart health and a foundation for love (Heartmath.com, 2016). The following examples will demonstrate the importance of giving for heart health.

A four-year-old boy had noticed a neighbor boy did not have many toys. He told his mother he wanted to give his three-wheel scooter to the boy. The mother walked with her son to the neighbors and said to the boy's father, "My son wants your son to have his three-wheel scooter." No one said a word as the four-year-old boy rolled the bike to the neighbor boy, lifted the rear seat to show where to store things, and then stepped back. The neighbor boy took the gift, sat on the seat, and smiled.

Next, an elderly man shared in a connection group at his church about a time when his three-year-old granddaughter had given him a big hug. Afterward, the child told him, "Grandpa, my heart is saying, 'Grandpa, Grandpa, Grandpa!'" The child tapped her chest in rhythm with her heartbeat. The man's eyes welled with tears of happiness as he recalled the event.

Exercising Your Heart, Mind, and Soul

Once you have mentally reconnected with, and acknowledged, your heart feelings, take a few minutes and accept them; agree with your feelings.

Perhaps you are hurt and sad at what someone did, something you did, or something that you didn't get and really wanted. Respect yourself and admit, "I feel hurt and sad. I feel hurt and sad. I feel hurt and sad." Give yourself a mental and physical hug.

Building Heart/Mind Connection

Free yourself and build your emotional resources by sending mental and heartfelt well-wishes to the one(s) you feel hurt you. This section describes an exercise you can do to increase your mental reserves and connections with your heart, and release emotional tensions. First, relax for a few minutes in a quiet place. If you don't have a quiet place, create a quiet place in your mind. Now think of someone for whom you have negative feelings.

In your mind imagine sending them positive feelings, sort of like the African Violet Lady giving away her flowers. Imagine sending this person positive heart emotions that will replace any negative ones you feel in your heart right now. For example, if you feel hurt and sad, say "I wish happiness and love for _____. I wish happiness and love for _____. I wish happiness and love for _____."

This mental exercise has been scientifically proven to grow one's brain by creating the capacity for more of the generous thoughts one gives away. The scientific reasoning behind this practice is called experience-dependent neuroplasticity (Forsyth, Bachman, Mathalon, Roach, and Asarnow, 2015). If you are imagining giving away good wishes for health, happiness, and well-being to another, the brain grows more of the capacity within itself for these qualities to compensate for what you gave.

You can help yourself, while helping others, by reconnecting with yourself and wishing goodwill to others. Improve your mental, physical, and spiritual health. The work of integration applies to all areas of your life. The healthier you want to be, the more you must reconnect with and manage your emotions, thoughts, and behaviors (Sherman and Cohen, 2006; Steele and Liu, 1983).

HEALTHY PRACTICES INVENTORY

Discover where you are in the use of healthy practices by taking the Healthy Practices Inventory in table 15.1.

Directions: Reflect on the following statements and rate yourself on how often you demonstrate these behaviors from 1 = Never to 6 = Always.

Table 15.1. Healthy practices inventory

Scale ratings	1	2	3	4	5	6
Items	Never	Irregularly	Occasionally	Frequently	Almost always	Always
1. I read uplifting and inspirational material, listen to advice from healthy others, and practice new ways for improving my behaviors						
2. I often remind myself that, if I put in the effort, I can grow and change						
3. I reflect on my behaviors and my thinking, compare them to a transcendent standard, and correct myself when I find I am wrong or behaving badly						
4. I eat natural whole foods and avoid processed foods						
5. I accept stress as my body's way of preparing for challenges and seek help from others when I feel stressed						
6. I wish good things for others and for myself, even when I feel hurt						
7. I give of my time and money to help others in need						
8. I am grateful for who I am, where I am, and others I know right now						

Calculating Your Score

Fill in the item scores on the following appropriate lines, sum, and divide the total by eight. This will give you the average score for all items:

Item 1 score _____
Item 2 score _____
Item 3 score _____
Item 4 score _____
Item 5 score _____
Item 6 score _____
Item 7 score _____
Item 8 score _____
Add scores _____/divide by 8 =_____ healthy processes score.

Understanding the Results

$x \leq 2.0$—Based on how you rated the items on the inventory, if your score is two or less, you have some room for improvement. Review which of the items from 1 to 8 are your lowest scores. You may have unresolved conflicts that weigh you down. Don't give up! Keep going. You are on the same road of life as everyone else and you can grow and learn if you put in the effort. You are valuable and have so much to give. You may not believe it, but your gift to others is uniquely yours, so stop looking at what others are doing and give your gift.

Stay open to find the good in yourself and in others around you. Seek healthy others and ask for someone you admire to mentor you on the way to developing a growth mindset. Pick one of the items in the list and begin to reflect and see what you can do to improve. Remember, practice is a part of learning, and it takes persistence over time to master any new skill. Review the *model of variables leading to successful goal attainment and feelings of happiness.* Begin to follow the steps. Best wishes to you always!

$2.1 \leq x \leq 4.0$—Based on how you rated the items on the inventory, you have an average level of healthy practices. You may have a fairly stable and supportive family and friends. However, if you are comfortable with the way you do things, and if you don't challenge yourself to grow and learn, you may decline in your health over time. Developing abundant health is an active process requiring effort. Don't settle for less.

As you read this book, look for ways you can build skills and a broader framework of how to integrate the variety of systems that you have in your body, mind, and spirit, with your behaviors. As you develop increasing integration, you will find you increase your healthy practices. You may find you can live life more fully by giving of yourself to help yourself and others grow and learn.

4.1 ≤ x ≤ 6—Congratulations! Based on how you rated the items on the scale, your healthy practices are high. A high score on this inventory suggests you have the ability to keep integrity with your mind, body, spirit, and behaviors. You participate in positive relationships, have a keen insight into complex social situations, most likely mentor others who come to you for help, and are grateful for the life you live.

Having healthy practices doesn't mean you have not encountered health problems in your life, or aren't experiencing some now. We are not in control of all the factors that influence our emotional, physical, and spiritual health. The key is to reach out and put in the effort to connect, learn from healthy others, reflect on transcendent values, and take care of oneself. Expand the transformative learning you have begun and bring your gifts to lift others. Doing this helps you too.

WHAT WE RESIST PERSISTS

The phrase *what you resist persists* captures the importance of making peace with our stressors physically, emotionally, and spiritually. Reflection is necessary for improved self-systems. The mind tends to isolate or reject problems in the body and psyche. We must make an effort to recognize those elements of ourselves with which we are at odds. Seek help to make corrections and develop healthy integration within the self.

Everyone needs to focus on taking care of themselves so they are able to help others. Be sure to take every opportunity to get enough sleep, play, physical activity, naturally healthy foods; balance your time between working toward your goals and just hanging out; and continue to develop and maintain healthy connections with healthy others (Rock, Siegel, Poelmans, and Payne, 2012, p. 3). Where you can, give a "blanket to someone living in a cold world."

Key points to remember

- Thinking that stress is harmful, rather than helpful, can increase your chance of dying.
- Expressing gratitude, making connections, and giving of yourself to others are three unsurprising things you can do to increase your well-being and happiness.

- Self-reflection and transcendent reflection provide ways to develop integrity within your multiple self-systems and can reduce internal conflicts and distress.
- A growth mindset is necessary to persist in the discipline required to master healthy practices.
- Never give up, keep going, you can do it by managing your mindset and maximizing your personal power to choose to grow and learn to be even healthier.

Chapter 16

Using the Research to Develop Growth

It is easier to build strong children than to repair broken men.

—Frederick Douglas, 1817–1895

A critical component of gaining mastery over one's experience in the world is understanding the intervention process that improves the accuracy of one's predictions and judgments. Once you understand the processes, you can help those you serve and lead to gain more control over their own implicit theories and skill development. Mindset interventions are designed to provide feedback and training to develop one's belief in the ability to change and grow.

New interventions have been researched and tested that helped students with their relationships in school, parents with family dynamics, reduced local crime, and more (Walton, 2014). Individual mindset interventions attempt to change the psychology of the individual and have been shown to improve one's behaviors. Group and organizational level interventions teach collaborative goal setting, shared leadership, and communication and support skills (Hanson, 2015 and 2017b).

Following are some explicit examples of mindset interventions.

MINDSET INTERVENTIONS

Individual Level

Consider the following interventions for developing improvements in an individual's social identity.

Parents, teachers, administrators, and leaders can provide opportunities for individuals to work in small groups including those with diverse individual makeups (gender, race, age, religious faith, performance levels, etc.). Individuals are shown to increase their sense of self-esteem when interactions are positive, because the time working together allows them to develop a team identity and reduces the fear of being rejected (Walton, 2014).

Affirming one's values—Give individuals the opportunity to write about their personal values. This type of personal affirmation has been shown to increase students' sense of integrity and self-control, and even resulted in weight loss (Walton, 2014).

Increasing personal sense of control—Structure the work, home, or school environment in ways that allow individuals choice over when to act independently or to engage socially in activities. By giving opportunities for choice, one's autonomy increases and this increases the sense of well-being (Hanson, 2017b; Walton, 2014).

Promoting one's sense of belonging—Create a network of psychological and social support for individuals to help manage their emotional fears and feelings of isolation. Supports may include formal sessions to orient new individuals to the ways of the system and to others in the work or school environment. Explain the processes, procedures, and whom to contact in the office, school, or other groups for various needs (Walton, 2014).

Be prepared to answer questions, give information on how to reach out for help. This is the area of offering a "blanket against a cold world" that reduces stress, improves well-being, and results in improved outcomes because individuals are relieved of stresses which allows more energy to focus on achieving their goals.

Believing others will value them—Individuals need to know they are valued for how they see themselves and that what they contribute to the group has value. Get to know the self-perceptions of those with whom you work and live, and acknowledge them. Find ways to match their skills, abilities, and interests with the jobs/tasks they do. Provide opportunities for others to choose how they might contribute to the group. Ask for feedback on whether the tasks that you are asking others to do have meaning to them (Hanson, 2015 and 2017b).

Dealing with one's memories of regressive learning—Suggest keeping journals and provide opportunities for individuals to write about memories of events connected with negative feelings, repeatedly over time. Research has shown this reduced the power of the memories, as evidenced by lower stress levels, improved immune strength, and fewer requests for medical help (Walton, 2014).

Group Level

This section is a review of the previous sections describing the activities of vital leadership toward developing group-level mindsets. Vital leaders use the resources to structure the formal systems at work, home, or school to ensure opportunities for meeting the needs of the individuals and group. Some interventions are similar at the group and system levels of organizing, such as providing training to individuals on how to work well together in groups; giving and receiving feedback; acknowledging contributions; providing activities that build team and organizational identity; and giving supportive feedback in a timely and positive fashion.

Group-level professional development for leaders, classroom teachers, employees in business, and athletic teams can explore additional interventions to

- support subordinates and peers in successful team work by identifying team goals that are useful and important to the organization's needs;
- reflect on their own propositions, being open to challenge their beliefs and research and inquire for new information to support improvements in perceptions;
- make changes, improvements, and revisions as a routine activity, not corrective;
- create a safe environment that is open to mistakes;
- don't make it personal;
- provide individuals with a voice and respond to their input (develop a sense of personal power within the team) (Hanson, 2015).

System Level

Rather than being the sum of individual beliefs, an organization's collectively held beliefs reflect the individuals' *shared beliefs about their organization.* Organizational learning requires changes at the system level to develop group mindset cultures through shared norms.

A list of research proven system interventions include

- changing the system schedule to support opportunities for teams to work together on a routine basis and develop organizational identities;
- providing routines within the work schedule to enable the entire workforce to collaborate, share knowledge, develop skills, and solve problems together, including collaborative decision making and shared leadership in areas that relate to system changes and employee development;
- understanding and sharing about how the mind works and respect for each individual's unique ways of seeing their world (mental maps);
- providing enough resources of time and materials to get the job done in a timely fashion;
- ensuring equity in responsibilities, predictability in the processes, accountability for non-normative behaviors, support for individuals and teams to ensure their needs are met within the workplace;

- explicitly teaching how to provide psychosocial support to those they lead (Brandstatter, Herrmann, and Schuler, 2013; Farrington et al., 2012; Hanson, 2017a).

Leadership activities, formal system structures, and the informal social relational structures in groups and organizations are not strictly separate constructs. All elements interact and create one experience; just as birds flock together, cooperate through common algorithms, and obtain safety and food for the individual well-being of all.

Modeling Transcendent Values

Vital leaders can support perceptions of organizational and procedural justice in their followers by modelling virtues, developing structures for equitable processes, and aligning the purposes of the organization with the individuals' goals. A variety of measures have been developed to help leaders in organizations collect data to measure one's performance in the area of ethical leadership.

The factors fit within an overarching ethical leadership framework that includes virtues, purpose, and practice (Lawton and Páez, 2014).

Figure 16.1 provides a comparison and contrast of the various factors of ethical leadership measures in the literature.

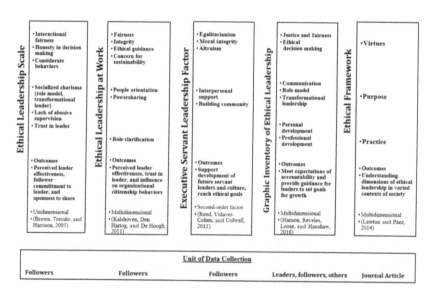

Figure 16.1. Map of comparable and contrasting concepts with ethical leadership constructs. *Source*: © Hanson, Loose, Reveles, and Hanshaw (2017).

INTERVENTION OUTCOMES

When leaders in companies use mindset interventions, worker satisfaction goes up, workers' perceptions of the culture go up, improvements in the ability to work together lead to innovations, social norms will develop, leading to increases in ethical behavior, and supervisors have a more positive view of employees (Delaney, Dweck, Murphy, Chatman, and Kray, 2015).

Use the framework from this book as a lens to create your own interventions and develop dialogues with others where you work and live. Review the previous models, or create your own models, about the processes you use to make your choices. Remember that a vital awareness and alignment of individual and group values are part of the cycle of developing shared social identities and trust at the system level.

MEASUREMENT TOOLS

Individual Mindset Scales

One can consider new ways to reflect and measure one's behaviors and perceptions toward developing a growth mindset. New measurement instruments have been developed to overcome response bias associated with traditional self-report surveys. This matter will be discussed in a later section on the criticisms of mindset theory. Figure 16.2 compares features of two new tools with Dweck's initial growth mindset survey in the domain of stability of one's intelligence.

Implicit Measurement Tool (IMT)

The IMT uses images and word association to quantify one's mindset belief toward intelligence as either stable or modifiable. The design of the IMT is intended to capture the subconscious associations as opposed to the individual's self-report of agreement with statements on a survey.

Implicit Relational Assessment Procedure (IRAP)

The IRAP uses word association to capture individuals' implicit beliefs avoiding measures of conscious self-reports (Power, Barnes-Holmes, Barnes-Holmes, and Stewart, 2009). It captures participant self-reports on; different types of goals, helplessness attributions, self-handicapping, disengagement, truancy, and grades of the participants.

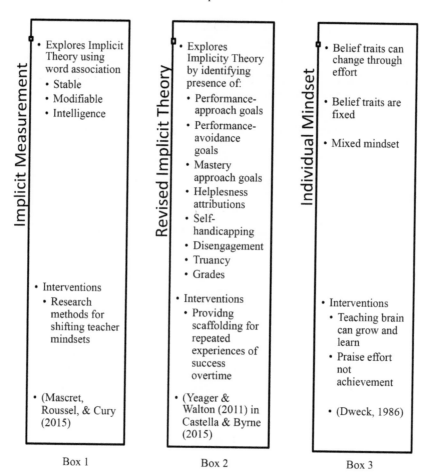

Figure 16.2. Comparison and contrast of Implicit Theory measurement tools.

Three Levels of Growth Mindset Measures

Most people familiar with the mindset concept have read about individual mindset. However, there are a variety of instruments for measuring the variables of a growth mindset at the individual, classroom/group, and organizational level. Figure 16.3 provides a model to compare the three levels of growth mindset constructs with each other and with variables found in organizational learning theories.

Individual Mindset Survey

The Individual Mindset Survey developed by Dweck (1986) seeks to quantify an individual's belief in the malleability of one's intelligence as either fixed or

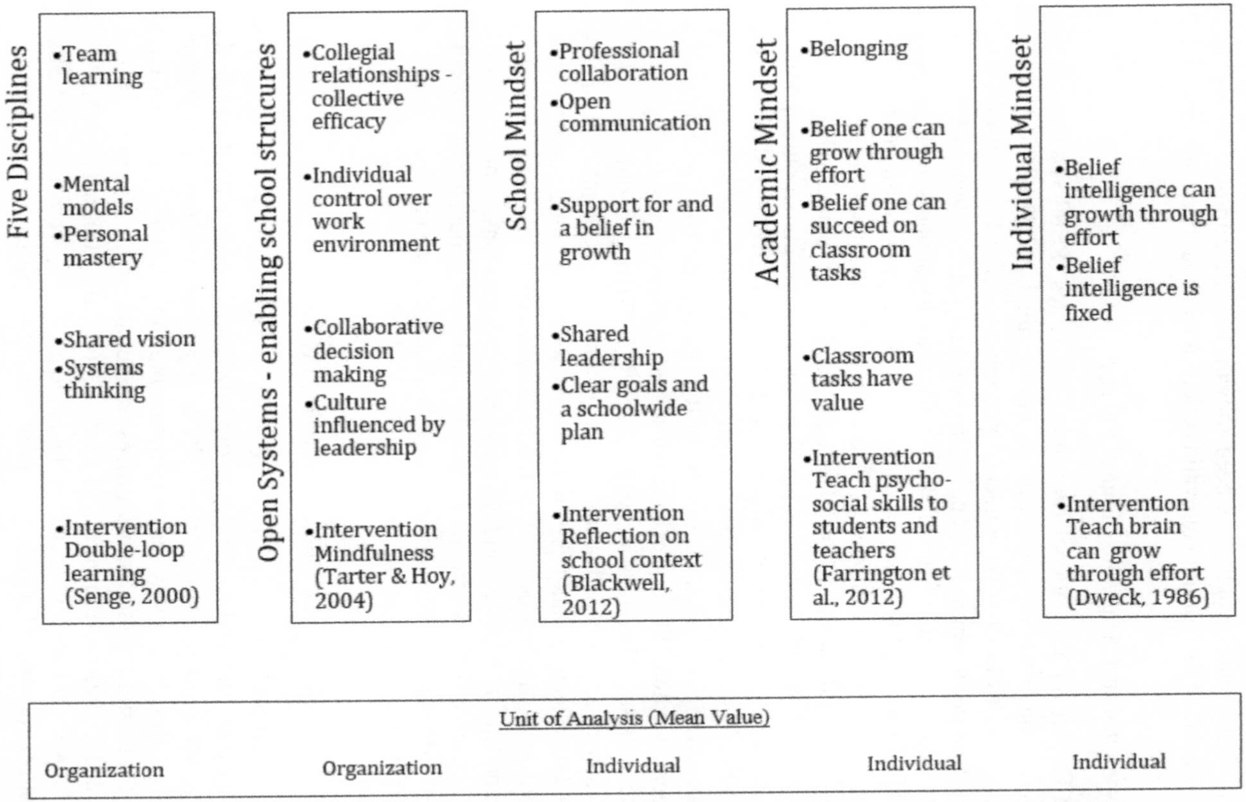

Five Disciplines
- Team learning
- Mental models
- Personal mastery
- Shared vision
- Systems thinking
- Intervention Double-loop learning (Senge, 2000)

Open Systems - enabling school structures
- Collegial relationships - collective efficacy
- Individual control over work environment
- Collaborative decision making
- Culture influenced by leadership
- Intervention Mindfulness (Tarter & Hoy, 2004)

School Mindset
- Professional collaboration
- Open communication
- Support for and a belief in growth
- Shared leadership
- Clear goals and a schoolwide plan
- Intervention Reflection on school context (Blackwell, 2012)

Academic Mindset
- Belonging
- Belief one can grow through effort
- Belief one can succeed on classroom tasks
- Classroom tasks have value
- Intervention Teach psycho-social skills to students and teachers (Farrington et al., 2012)

Individual Mindset
- Belief intelligence can growth through effort
- Belief intelligence is fixed
- Intervention Teach brain can grow through effort (Dweck, 1986)

Unit of Analysis (Mean Value)

Organization	Organization	Individual	Individual	Individual

Figure 16.3. Model of comparable and contrasting concepts with mindset constructs. *Source:* © Hanson (2015).

growth. In more recent studies a mixed mindset has also been discussed. This individual mindset survey is found in a variety of forms and lengths. A short version (four item length) has been shown, through empirical testing, to be less reliable in use for drawing valid conclusions about one's mindset beliefs.

Classroom-Level Academic Mindset Survey

The Project for Educational Research That Scales (PERTS) survey is used for collecting data about students' academic mindsets. The survey provides four subscales to discover students' perceptions related to: self-efficacy on classroom tasks, sense of belonging in the classroom, relevance of classroom tasks, and one's individual belief about the stability of one's intelligence. The PERTS instrument provides baseline data to track growth toward developing positive psychosocial supports for students in the classroom.

A mean calculated at the classroom level can provide reliable data to compare a teacher's purported practices and how the classroom supports are experienced by the students. Significant differences have been shown in average PERTS classroom scores between elementary and secondary levels and between various demographics. The PERTS can be used as a boundary object to identify where differences in mean scores exist between subcategories and contexts in schools (Hanson, 2017a, b; PERTS, 2016a, 2016b).

Teachers and school leaders can begin the process of mindset interventions by collecting data-based information about individual, classroom, and school-level mindset belief. Use the data evidence to allow students, teachers, and leaders to reflect and challenge their assumptions. A next step would be to observe what is actually happening, and finally, develop agreement on interventions uniquely useful to the individual, classroom, and school contexts (Murphy and Dweck, 2010; Hanson, 2017b).

School Growth Mindset Culture Survey (WMSM)

Recall that building a vital awareness of the deeply held values of those in the organization and aligning the organizational goals with the individuals' goals and roles is a prerequisite to a growth mindset organizational culture. Building awareness requires obtaining reliable research-based data for beginning the inquiry process and challenging assumptions (Hanson, 2015, Hanson, Bangert, and Ruff, 2016; Ruff, 2002). The *What's My School Mindset* survey, found on the Mindset Works website, may be used to collect reliable data about a school's mindset culture.

The faculty can use the data collected from their own self-reports to challenge their perceptions (espoused beliefs) by making observations about what is actually happening (theories in practice) in the school and comparing the results. Use the results to collaborate together and develop context-specific interventions and a plan to reach aligned goals for the growth and well-being of all involved (Hanson, Bangert, and Ruff, 2016).

Ethical Leadership Measurement Scale

The Graphic Inventory of Ethical Leadership (GIEL) scale identifies three categories of ethical leadership behaviors. Measurement scales may be used by universities with their candidates in administrator services credential programs. Leaders, administrators, and managers can use the survey to obtain data on how others view them, self-reflect, set goals for improvement, and track growth.

The GIEL captures data on administrator's ethical behaviors by asking participants to rate the frequency of observed behaviors of the leader in the following areas identified from the literature, and in national and state standards

- Justice and equitable decision making
- Communication and modeling
- Personal and professional development. (Hanson, Loose, Reveles, and Hanshaw, 2017)

Leaders model behaviors that can be internalized by the followers as norms of organizational behavior. When leaders demonstrate ethical behaviors, followers develop trust, which may lead to organizational citizenship behaviors and collective efficacy, and increase the well-being and vitality of the individuals and organization.

Vital leaders must have transformative learning, skills as a manager, and a growth mindset in order to be effective role models. As previously shared, research revealed when leaders believed in the potential for growth, their followers increased their trust in the leader. Leaders with growth mindsets also thought more highly of their employees (Delaney, Dweck, Murphy, Chatman, and Kray, 2015).

CRITICISMS OF THE MINDSET THEORY

A thorough understanding of any concept benefits from a review of the limitations and delimitations of the research on mindset. Following is a discussion of a review of relevant literature on this topic.

Fixedness of Mindset Categories

Dweck's individual mindset survey research used brief questionnaires to collect individuals' beliefs about the changeability of their intelligence. The researchers divided the results into data ranges and assigned a label of fixed to the low range and growth to the high range. Researchers separated the individuals into categories based upon the mean score calculated from their scale responses.

Concerns raised by other researchers considered growth mindset theory to be a "reductionistic measurement model." Reductionist means the constructs of fixed, growth, and neither mindsets are created and do not represent all the potentials that exist in individual beliefs along a continuum (Collinson and Cook, 2007; Ogden, 2003).

Accuracy of Scales

Researchers have historically challenged the accuracy of the scales purported to measure abstract social science constructs, such as the construct of fixed and growth mindset. One recommendation researchers made to capture participant's perceptions accurately was to create definitions for observed behaviors. The rating scale for observed behaviors would be for observed frequency of the behaviors, rather than Likert-type scales of one's agreement or disagreement to an item.

Validity of Construct

Mindset researchers have used labels of fixed and growth to explain variations in individuals' choices and behaviors purported to result from the participants' beliefs. Isolating the individual's underlying motivations for his or her actions is difficult. Measurement tools that purport to capture a certain abstract idea, such as mindset, continue to be challenged.

Researchers studying the measurement of values-based behaviors explained that certain behaviors can be motived by a variety of values that may conflict with one another. For example, participating in a worthy cause may be motivated by a belief in the cause as well as a desire for social approval. Often individuals are unaware of their motivations or are biased in their thinking (Lönnqvist, Verkasalo, Wichardt, and Walkowitz, 2013).

Researchers have suggested avoiding the measurement of values shown to have confounding influences that cannot be untangled. They explain it is difficult to ensure the construct one purports to measure is actually the one participants have in mind when responding to items on a self-report scale.

Priming Influence of the Research Process

Some researchers questioned whether the mindset research process, such as asking participants to complete questionnaires, influenced the participants' views (priming) and affected the results of the study (Ogden, 2003). For example, in one study when students became aware of the purpose of the mindset research interventions the results were compromised.

Incomplete Representation of Factors

Other factors relevant to the development and maintenance of mindset constructs, such as goal setting and goal attainment, were not addressed in some growth mindset research (Plaks, Grant, and Dweck, 2005). Recent research in this area has begun to address this issue revealing the importance of the goal alignment process in promoting a growth mindset culture.

Usefulness of Interventions

Early studies using mindset interventions at the individual mindset level showed less potential for generating improvement than those focused at the level of the organization. Improvements in student outcomes were usually limited to students with low performance, of a minority race, or of the female gender (Aronson, Cohen, and McColskey, 2009).

Also, research for individual mindset interventions often used small sample sizes and showed only modest gains (on average .3 GPA points) for only subcategories of the student population (Farrington et al., 2012, p. 36). New studies are being carried out at scale, showing promise for new psychosocial interventions across a variety of demographics (Yeager et al., 2014).

For example, one study explored the parents' influence on their children's mindset as a result of the parents' responses to the child's failures (Haimovitz and Dweck, 2016; Heyman and Dweck, 1998). Another study, with students in Chile, revealed low-income students with individual growth mindsets were outperforming students from more well-to-do backgrounds, who expressed fixed mindsets (Claro, Paunesku, and Dweck, 2016; Dweck, 2016).

Domain Specific Nature

Mindset is actually a domain-specific construct. This means a person's or group's mindset may vary depending on the area being evaluated. One can have a growth mindset about one's intelligence and a fixed mindset about one's athletic ability. Each belief is influenced by the individual's monitoring of feedback in the context of the situation.

One's mindset can be shifted by influencing a variety of malleable factors in one's environment, challenging ones assumptions, observing others model a growth mindset, and experiencing repeated positive experiences in a supportive environment.

ALTERNATIVE THEORIES

For readers interested in understanding the breadth of psychosocial theories similar to the concept of growth and fixed mindset, a variety of alternative theories as well as theories expanding on the mindset concept are provided next.

Bandura's (1986, 1988, 2001) work in social cognitive theory is a foundational concept in mindset theory. The concept of individual agency within SCT is also foundational to the concept of a growth mindset as well as to Bandura's self-efficacy and collective efficacy models. Dweck performed research studies at Stanford University where Bandura also performed his influential work.

Dweck and Leggett's (1988) goal theory, Kirshner and Whitson's (1998) situated learning, and Senge's mental models and Five Disciplines (1990) all viewed individual agency and learner choice over goals as crucial elements contributing to meaningful learning, also described by Novak (2002) and Novak and Gowin (1984).

Hong, Chiu, Dweck, Lin, and Wan's (1999) *meaning system approach* and the setting, operating, monitoring, and attainment model incorporated theories from mindset research. Researchers explored the influence of implicit theories such as mindset on the feedback loop in goal attainment through self-regulation. Individuals' implicit (growth mindset) theories explained the ability to self-regulate and to gain progress toward goals (Burnette, O'Boyle, Vanepps, Pollack, and Finkel, 2013), and Gollwitzer (1990) added to the literature by describing goal theory.

Gollwitzer's research focused on two stages in the goal attainment process, decision making and implementation, instead of one's beliefs about one's intelligence. The implicit learning theories of Burnette, O'Boyle, Vanepps, Pollack, and Finkel (2013) suggested that the content and structure of one's memory differed depending on one's level of awareness and the purpose of one's motives or goals.

Key points to remember

- New interventions have been developed that help individuals recognize and overcome biases and errors in their thinking so they can improve and grow.

- Interventions at the individual level attempt to change the psychology of the individual.
- Group and system interventions teach collaborative goal setting, shared leadership, and skills for communicating and providing support to others in the group.
- A variety of measurement scales have been developed and tested to quantify individual, group, and organizational culture growth mindset factors.
- Vital leaders within open vital systems provide transformational leadership and managerial leadership, values-based systems, and processes that promote improved connections, power of personal choice, and shared meaning making.

Chapter 17

Putting It All Together

Every moment makes a contribution, every little detail plays a part. Having just the vision's no solution, everything depends on execution. Putting it together, that's what counts.

—Stephen Sondheim, *Sunday in the Park with George*

A growth mindset is a theory of mind set in a framework of autonomous flexible action. Autonomy, the power of personal choice, comes from developing resilience and skills to move between social integration and independent action. A growth mindset is a key part of the human ability to make sense of the world, without which individuals limit their willingness to receive and give feedback in a recursive cycle. A growth mindset contributes to one's ability to adapt to meet the demands of a changing and complex world.

Both internal stories and the external physical and social environmental factors are sources of feedback. Negative feedback may result in a shift to a fixed mindset. An individual with a fixed mindset belief may internalize a growth mindset when participating in a group that has a growth mindset culture. Belief in one's inability to grow and learn may be a realistic reflection of the experiences one has in an unsupported or unsafe environment, and a reasonable safeguard to protect one from threats to one's self-image and from harm in unhealthy situations.

DEVELOPING OUR INDIVIDUAL IDENTITY

Individuals shape their perceptions of their individual identities through learning. One can expand the boundaries of "self" through interactions with others in safe and supported social contexts. One's family, faith group, or others with lifetime commitments support and protect the welfare of the individual through their intimate long-term social relationships.

The individual learns how to present himself or herself socially and to respect others' unique representations of their world through these social involvements; two critical skills needed to act successfully in society. As the individual matures, he or she develops broader experiences in a social context with the community, school, and clubs.

This expanding awareness of others develops a social identity that can be described through an analogy of birds flocking together. Simple social rules (norms, algorithms) define the relationships and actions of the individuals in these groups. In the expanding social context, individuals do not require as deep a social identification as was necessary in the primary units of identity development.

As an individual moves through life's experiences, he or she develops a unique view of his or her world and creates stories that give meaning to his or her experiences. When these stories are aligned with the stories of healthy others, bonding connections can result supporting the individuals' individual identities and creating a deeper social identity and commitment to a collective experience.

Experiences with diverse others, whose experiences and stories are different, can challenge one's sense of identity. Vital leaders are necessary to act as proxy agents when individuals reach "boundaries" of their self-knowledge and skills of how to act with diverse others. Processes of open vital systems include putting context-specific scaffolds into place in the formal structures of systems to create safety, equity, and predictability.

Vital leaders shape formal structures that support opportunities to develop bridging connections between individuals in the organization when social identification does not occur, and motivate others to higher standards. Individuals can reflect on their thinking and actions for the purpose of improving the accuracy of their mental models (Ruff, 2002). Individuals with a vital awareness feel connected to and value a broader range of others.

Just as we will always experience stress (the body's preparation to meet challenges), we will also feel a measure of loneliness (the sense of our body as separate from others, the "I"). Our mindset influences the choices we make to respond to these feelings. Social support is necessary for individual emotional self-regulation and for overcoming the psychological and social traumas many people in society are experience.

WORKING TOGETHER IN A SOCIAL CONTEXT

The use of transcendent referents for reflection and correction can result in a vital awareness of one's responsibility for one's actions and relationships toward self, others, the world, and the transcendent source. The analogy of a pseudopodia, a collection of individual sea animals working together by providing a protective coating that enables them to increase their ability to survive, may be used to describe processes of a mature social organization.

Mature individuals contribute resources and psychosocial supports to help others develop, providing a "blanket against a cold world."

Individuals seek help from others to accomplish their goals through a process called proxy agency. Proxy agency can occur in a one-to-one relationship or collectively. Collective action results in collective agency if the system's formal processes and goals align with the individuals' goals and needs. When this occurs the needs and goals of the individuals are said to be contextualized, which means to be consistent with the purpose of organizing.

Vital leaders use transformational leadership to demonstrate procedural justice and model a growth mindset motivating the followers to higher levels of awareness and cognitive development. When individuals feel they will receive a benefit from others with whom they live and work, and that they will not be harmed, trust results. Trust is a necessary ingredient to open vital systems organizational learning, and leads to flexibility.

One's culture of origin influences one's worldview. Generally, Eastern and Western worldviews lead to different mindset orientations on a continuum of fixed to growth. This may vary at the individual level. In Western cultures, such as the United States and European countries, the emphasis on independence contributes to a fundamental attribution error that may overlook the influence of the social context on one's choices and lead to inaction.

The development of a vital self-awareness contributes to the power to act in integrity with one's values in spite of influences to the contrary. We need just processes in systems to protect us from self-interested behaviors of others and our own self-interest. Healthy human social organization is the result of developing commonly shared memories of expected behaviors (norms) for the group.

People organize for different reasons and those reasons influence the development of socially accepted behaviors in the group. When market norms prevail, individuals seek equal value or advantage over the other in their exchanges. Under conditions of social norms, individuals contribute to the success and smooth operations of the group without expecting an immediate return.

A growth mindset culture promotes healthy social norms. However, informal hierarchies may use political means and seek to control the resources and actions of the group for self-interest rather than the well-being of those in the system and in society. The rule of law and legitimate use of force is intended to create a balance of power and protections for those with fewer social, economic, or physical resources.

Researchers have identified a variety of transcendent values that hold true across time and culture and contribute to the welfare of all. One develops wisdom and maturity through making the personal choice to reflect on one's biases and errors, using transcendent referents to correct one's actions, and through acting on a belief in the potential for growth in self and others.

THE INFLUENCE OF SELF-SYSTEMS

Language System

The way we use language can contribute to improved understanding or misunderstandings between the speaker and the listener(s). The sorites paradox is an exploration of errors in communication that can occur when using abstractions (words that label ideas as if they are concrete objects). Fixed mindsets can develop through thinking of the abstract idea of intelligence as a trait.

We can promote the development of growth mindsets in ourselves and others by being selective with the words we use to think and communicate, such as praising effort rather than traits, or encouraging progress over time rather than immediate accomplishments and grades.

The Mind, Body, and Soul

The mind and the brain work together to build patterns for how we will behave. A growth mindset belief contributes to openness to reflect on one's thinking and make appropriate corrections. Understanding the functions of the brain helps one appreciate the importance of developing integration in all the processes including; our body, mind, and soul systems.

Accepting oneself and being open to change is crucial to healthy integration. One needs internalized transcendent values to maximize one's power of personal choice and contribute to one's individual and social well-being. Well-being and *individual happiness* are vague terms. A list of factors suggested by researchers included; one's satisfaction with life, the meanings we give our memories, nature of one's actual experiences, and one's positive functioning.

Our greatest health, well-being, and happiness come from being able to contribute to others in a mutual connection. Happiness is not an outcome, or something one gets, but the experience of healthy connectedness that comes from sustained, frequent, positive interactions over time. Participating in social settings requires high cognitive skills, because of the complexity of working with diverse others.

CONTRIBUTING TO GROWTH

As society changes from the introduction of advancing technologies, advocates suggest the tremendous advantages to create efficient and effective processes. Efficiency and effectiveness are not goals but means to goals. The individual ought never to be equated with tools nor used as a means. Rather, all policy and practices can be judged in the light of how they affect the overall welfare of others. Therefore, efficiency and effectiveness must serve higher moral values, be subsumed, under practices that provide for and protect the well-being of all.

One's beliefs about the ability to grow and learn influence the goals one chooses and strategies to reach them. Few people can reach their goals independently, that is, without help, support, or resources from anyone else. A growth mindset is needed for learning how to correct and develop our mental representations of our experiences and for understanding that others' perceptions and ideas may differ from our own.

As we develop a vital awareness, we can choose different outcomes to measure, including individual well-being, just as the country of Bhutan has chosen to shift its focus from GNP to GNH. As individuals it is imperative that we meet the ethical mandate to develop a collective sense of "we" and develop systems that provide safety and liberty with legitimate goals aligned with the individuals' needs.

Individuals come together to improve and grow. Through processes of relational learning we increase our skills, and increase the accuracy of our cognitive processes for predicting and responding to new circumstances. Societies can be developed and shaped by individuals coming together to create open vital systems that protect the liberties of the individuals within them as we meet life's challenges together.

MINDSET AT THE CENTER OF THE LOVS FRAMEWORK

Figure 17.1 shows a cycle of variables related to managing your mindset set in the LOVS framework. Each box in the cycle reflects one aspect of the social processes used in your home, classroom, school, workplace, or teams. Use the model to reflect and challenge your own assumptions and behaviors. Select one box at a time and inquire further about the concepts in the box.

For example, take some time to look over the items listed in the System Behavior Styles box. Consider whether your behaviors in the group, and your group's behaviors, are most similar to an

- erratic style, where individual identities predominate (useful for high individual creativity);
- systematic style, where rules and structures direct most of the behaviors (useful in stable and predictable environments such as a factory);
- organic style, where highly specialized activities require high skills and precision to work together as teams (example may be processes used in a

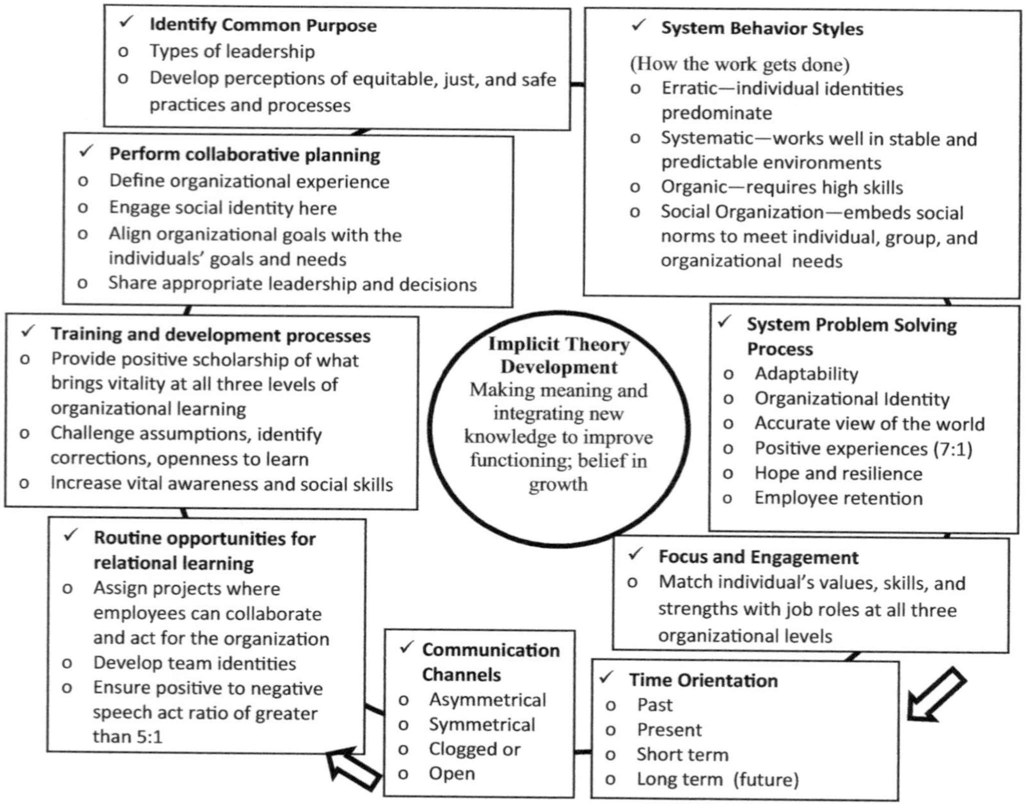

✓ Identify Common Purpose
o Types of leadership
o Develop perceptions of equitable, just, and safe practices and processes
✓ System Behavior Styles
(How the work gets done)
o Erratic—individual identities predominate
o Systematic—works well in stable and predictable environments
o Organic—requires high skills
o Social Organization—embeds social norms to meet individual, group, and organizational needs
✓ Perform collaborative planning
o Define organizational experience
o Engage social identity here
o Align organizational goals with the individuals' goals and needs
o Share appropriate leadership and decisions
✓ Training and development processes
o Provide positive scholarship of what brings vitality at all three levels of organizational learning
o Challenge assumptions, identify corrections, openness to learn
o Increase vital awareness and social skills
Implicit Theory Development
Making meaning and integrating new knowledge to improve functioning; belief in growth
✓ System Problem Solving Process
o Adaptability
o Organizational Identity
o Accurate view of the world
o Positive experiences (7:1)
o Hope and resilience
o Employee retention
✓ Routine opportunities for relational learning
o Assign projects where employees can collaborate and act for the organization
o Develop team identities
o Ensure positive to negative speech act ratio of greater than 5:1
✓ Focus and Engagement
o Match individual's values, skills, and strengths with job roles at all three organizational levels
✓ Communication Channels
o Asymmetrical
o Symmetrical
o Clogged or
o Open
✓ Time Orientation
o Past
o Present
o Short term
o Long term (future)

Figure 17.1. Model of implicit theory development in a framework of leadership within open vital systems.

hospital, like a model of a living cell where each part has autonomy to perform a highly specialized function) (Gilbert and Gilbert, 1995); or

- a social organization, using healthy social norms to allow flexible structures and the ability for relational learning (needed when flexibly and adaptability are required to find solutions in rapidly changing and complex situations such as within a family, diverse school populations, or community; in multi-national communications, and multi-national corporations).

Inquire further into the model to explore ways you can intervene and develop yourself and your group for improved functioning and a growth mindset. Discuss and challenge your assumptions. Be flexible; each model of organizing is useful in the correct context.

Reflection is the first step in the process for understanding the factors/variables that contribute to the development of a growth mindset. As you explore further, consider using some of the variety of tools researchers have developed to measure mindset at the individual, group/classroom, and organizational culture levels. Use the data to engage in conversations about your perceptions and what is actually happening in your home, school, or anywhere you work or live.

A variety of interventions have been described in the literature to help individuals overcome regressive learning and develop productive learning. Psychosocial supports are a significant piece of the process for developing a growth mindset in individuals and a growth mindset culture in organizations. Individuals and leaders can work together to promote a belief in the ability that everyone they love, lead, and serve can grow and learn.

Bandura (2001) warned of the importance of developing accurate understandings and high skills to engage through collective efficacy and meet the challenges of an emergent information technology age. Advances in technologies, communication, information systems, and transportation have changed the way society operates. Digital media do not replace the need for human touch, time together to develop shared understanding and trust, and to give and receive support.

Recall our ability to determine our own goals and act collectively to achieve them relies on the management of our learning, the careful selection of the data we receive, and the judgments we assign to it.

CONCLUSION

This book has been written to provide a framework for your use in creating *new meanings* that are uniquely yours. You can further develop your understanding of mindset and the power of personal choice through inviting others you know to join in an inquiry of your world through the lens of the growth mindset framework provided here. Having done your part in reading this book, you can begin to manage your own mindset and maximize your power of personal choice to bring you farther along your path today than you were before.

I wish the best for you always.

Bibliography

Achor, S. (2011, May). The happy secret to better work (Video file). Retrieved from https://www.ted.com/talks/shawn_achor_the_happy_secret_to_better_work/transcript?language=en#t-6000

Akkerman, S. F., & Bakker, A. (2011). Boundary crossing and boundary objects. *Review of Educational Research, 81*(2), 132–169. http://doi.org/10.3102/0034654311404435

Alexander, B. K. (2008). *The globalisation of addiction: A study in poverty of the spirit*. New York, NY: Oxford University Press, Inc.

Alexander, B. K. (2010). Addiction: The view from Rat Park (2010). Rat Park. Retrieved June 1, 2017, from http://www.brucekalexander.com/articles-speeches/rat-park/148-addiction-the-view-from-rat-park

"The Analects" as reported in *Chambers Dictionary of Quotations* (1997). London, UK: Chambers. Wikiquotes. Retrieved from https://en.wikiquote.org/wiki/Confucius

Appel, G. (November 20, 2016). This is for everyone—week 1. *Full Service | Podcast*. Eastside Christian Church. Available at http://www.eastside.com/thisisforeveryone#thisisforeveryonecontent

Archie, E. A., and Tung, J. (2015). Social behavior and the microbiome. *Current Opinion in Behavioral Sciences, 6,* 28–34. http://doi.org/10.1016/j.cobeha.2015.07.008

Ariely, D. (2008). *Predictably irrational*. New York, NY: Harper Collins.

Ariely, D. (2012). *The (honest) truth about dishonesty*. New York, NY: Harper Collins.

Aronson, J., Cohen, G., and McColskey, W. (2009). Reducing stereotype threat in classrooms: A review of social-psychological intervention studies on improving the achievement of black students (Regional Education Laboratory, REL 2009-086). National Center for Education Evaluation and Regional Assistance, Institute for Education Science, U.S. Department of Education.

Asimov, I. (2017). Good Reads. Retrieved from http://www.goodreads.com/author/quotes/16667.Isaac_Asimov

Aslan, M., Beycioglu, K., and Konan, N. (2008). Principals' openness to change in Malatya, Turkey. *International Electronic Journal for Leadership in Learning, 12*(8), 8. Retrieved from http://files.eric.ed.gov/fulltext/EJ940565.pdf

Attenborough, R., and Gandhi, M. K. (1982). *The words of Gandhi.* New York, NY: New Market Press.

Bandura, A. (1977). *Social learning theory.* Englewood Cliffs, NJ: Prentice Hall.

Bandura, A. (1986). *Social foundations of thought and action: A social cognitive theory.* Englewood Cliffs, NJ: Prentice-Hall.

Bandura, A. (1988). Organizational application of social cognitive theory. *Australian Journal of Management, 13*(2), 275–302. http://doi.org/10.1177/031289628801300210

Bandura, A. (1989a). Human agency in social cognitive theory. *American Psychologist, 44*(9), 1175–1184. http://doi.org/10.1037/0003-066X.44.9.1175. PMID 2782727.

Bandura, A. (1989b). Regulation of cognitive processes through perceived self-efficacy. *Developmental Psychology, 25*(5), 729–735. https://doi.org/10.1037/0012-1649.25.5.729

Bandura, A. (1989c). Social cognitive theory. In R. Vasta (Ed.), *Annals of child development, 6.* Six theories of child development (pp. 1–60). Greenwich, CT: JAI Press.

Bandura, A. (1994). Self-efficacy. In V. S. Ramachaudran (Ed.), *Encyclopedia of human behavior 4* (pp. 71–81). New York: Academic Press. (Reprinted in H. Friedman [Ed.], *Encyclopedia of mental health.* San Diego: Academic Press, 1998).

Bandura, A. (1997). *Self-efficacy: The exercise of control.* New York: Freeman.

Bandura, A. (2001). Social cognitive theory: An agentic perspective. *Annual Review of Psychology, 52,* 1–26. https://doi.org/10.1146/annurev.psych.52.1.1

Bandura, A. (2002). Social cognitive theory in cultural context. *Applied Psychology, 51*(2), 269–290. https://doi.org/10.1111/1464-0597.00092

Bandura, A. (2011). The social and policy impact of social cognitive theory. In M. Mark, S. Donaldson, and B. Campbell (Eds.), *Social psychology and evaluation* (pp. 33–70). New York, NY: Guilford Press.

Batson, C. D., & Shaw, L. L. (1991). Evidence for altruism: Toward a pluralism of prosocial motives. Psychological Inquiry, 2(2), 107–122.

Baumeister, R., Masicampo, E., and Vohs, K. (2011). Do conscious thoughts cause behavior? *Annual Review of Psychology, 62*(1), 331–361. http://doi.org/10.1146/annurev.psych.093008.131126

Berber, A., and Rofcanin, Y. (2012). Investigation of organization citizenship behavior construct a framework for antecedents and consequences. *International Journal of Business and Social Research (IJBSR), 2*(4), 195–210. https://doi.org/10.18533/ijbsr.v2i4.221

Bierstedt, R. (1981). *American sociological theory: A critical history.* New York, NY: Academic Press, Inc.

Blackwell, L. (2012, March 28). Developing a growth mindset school culture. *Mindset Works' Blog: Cultivating Growth Mindsets.* Retrieved October 26, 2016, from http://blog.mindset works.com/blog-page/home-blogs/entry/developing-a-growth-mindset-school-culture-2-ar

Blackwell, L. S., Trzesniewski, K. H., and Dweck, C. S. (2007). Implicit theories of intelligence predict achievement across an adolescent transition: A longitudinal study and an intervention. *Child Development, 78,* 246–263, Study 1. https://doi.org/10.1111/j.1467-8624.2007.00995.x

Bolino, M. C., Turnley, W. H., and Bloodgood, J. M. (2002). Citizenship behavior and the creation of social capital in organizations. *Academy of management review, 27*(4), 505–522.

Boomer, L. G. (2012). Leadership, management and administration: What's the difference? *Accounting Today, 26*(9), 34. Retrieved from https://search.proquest.com/docview/1041052931?accountid=8459

Boulding, K. E. (n.d.). General systems theory. Retrieved October 9, 2016, from http://www.hofkirchner.uti.at/wp-content/uploads/2010/10/GSTcombined.pdf.

Brandstatter, V., Herrmann, M., and Schuler, J. (2013). The struggle of giving up personal goals: Affective, physiological, and cognitive consequences of an action crisis. *Personality and Social Psychology Bulletin, 39*(12), 1668–1682. https://doi.org/10.1177/0146167213500151

Bregman, R. (2017, April). Poverty isn't a lack of character; it's a lack of cash. [Video file]. Retrieved from https://www.ted.com/talks/rutger_bregman_poverty_isn_t_a_lack_of_character_it_s_a_lack_of_cash/transcript?language=en

Brown, M. E., Treviño, L. K., and Harrison, D. A. (2005). Ethical leadership: A social learning perspective for construct development and testing. *Organizational Behavior and Human Decision Processes, 97*(2), 117–134. https://doi.org/10.1016/j.obhdp.2005.03.002

Burcharth, A. L., and Fosfuri, A. (2015). Not invented here: How institutionalized socialization practices affect the formation of negative attitudes toward external knowledge. *Industrial and Corporate Change, 24*(2), 281–305. https://doi.org/10.1093/icc/dtu018

Burke Harris, N. (2015, February). How childhood trauma affects health across a lifetime (Video file). Retrieved from https://www.ted.com/talks/nadine_burke_harris_how_childhood_trauma_affects_health_across_a_lifetime/transcript?language=en

Burnette, J. L., O'Boyle, E. H., Vanepps, E. M., Pollack, J. M., and Finkel, E. J. (2013). Mind-sets matter: A meta-analytic review of implicit theories and self-regulation. *Psychological Bulletin, 139*(3), 655–701. https://doi.org/10.1037/a0029531

Burns, L. C. (1991). *Vagueness: An investigation into natural languages and the sorites paradox.* University of Melbourne, Australia: Springer Science + Business Media B. V.

Cameron, W. B. (1963). *Informal sociology, a casual introduction to sociological thinking.* New York, NY: Random House. Retrieved from http://quoteinvestigator.com/2010/05/26/everything-counts-einstein/

Cardenas, D., (2013). Let not thy food be confused with thy medicine: The Hippocratic misquotation, *e-SPEN Journal,* http://doi.org/10.1016/j.clnme.2013.10.002

Carlin, R. E., and Love, G. J. (2013). The politics of interpersonal trust and reciprocity: An experimental approach. *Political Behavior, 35,* 43–63. http://doi:10.1007/s11109-011-9181-x

Chaplain, W. F., John, O. P., and Goldberg L. R. (1988). Conceptions of states and traits: Dimensional attributes with ideals as prototypes. *Journal of Personality and Social Psychology, 54*(4), 541–557. https://doi.org/10.1037/0022-3514.54.4.541

Chirkov, V., Ryan, R. M., Kim, Y., and Kaplan, U. (2003). Differentiating autonomy from individualism and independence: A self-determination theory perspective on internalization of cultural orientations and well-being. *Journal of Personality and Social Psychology, 84*(1), 94–110. https://doi.org/10.1037/0022-3514.84.1.97

Choi, I., Nisbett, R. E., and Norenzayan, A. (1999). Causal attribution across cultures: Variation and universality. *Psychological Bulletin, 125*(1), 47–63. https://doi.org/10.1037/0033-2909.125.1.47

Claro, S., Paunesku, D., and Dweck, C. S. (2016). Growth mindset tempers the effects of poverty on academic achievement. *Proceedings of the National Academy of Sciences of the United States of America, 113*(31), 8664–8668. https://doi.org/10.1073/pnas.1608207113

Clews-De Castella, K., and Byrne, D. (2015). My intelligence may be more malleable than yours: The revised implicit theories of intelligence (self-theory) scale is a better predictor of achievement, motivation, and student disengagement. *European Journal of Psychology of Education, 30*(3), 245–267. https://doi.org/10.1007/s10212-015-0244-y

Cloud, H. (2011). *The secret of happiness*. New York, NY: Howard Books.

Collinson, V., and Cook, T. F. (2007). *Organizational learning: Improving learning, teaching, and leading in school systems*. Thousand Oaks, CA: Sage.

Courtney, H. S., Navarro, E., and O'Hare, C.A. (2007). The dynamic organic transformational (D.O.T.) team model for high-performance knowledge-worker teams. *Team Performance Management: An International Journal, 13*(1), 34–46. http://doi.org/10.1108/13527590710736716

Dai, T., and Cromley, J. (2014). Changes in implicit theories of ability in biology and dropout from STEM majors: A latent growth curve approach. *Contemporary Educational Psychology, 39*(3), 233–247. http://doi.org/10.1016/j.cedpsych.2014.06.003

Darwin, C. R. (1859). *The origin of species (vol. XI)*. The Harvard Classics. New York, NY: P. F. Collier and Son, 1909–1914.

DeGroot, T., and Brownlee, A. L. (2006). Effect of department structure on the organizational citizenship behavior-department effectiveness relationship. *Journal of Business Research, 59*, 1116–1123. http://doi.org/10.1016/j.jbusres.2006.09.020

Delaney, S., Dweck, C., Murphy, M., Chatman, J., and Kray, L. (2015, January 1). New study findings: Why fostering a growth mindset in organizations matters. Retrieved June 30, 2017 from http://knowledge.senndelaney.com/docs/thought_papers/pdf/stanford_agilitystudy_hart.pdf

Den Hartog, D. N., Van Muijen, J. J., and Koopman, P. L. (1997). Transactional versus transformational leadership: An analysis of the MLQ. *Journal of Occupational and Organizational Psychology, 70*, 19–34. http://doi.org/10.1111/j.2044-8325.1997.tb00628.x

Descartes, R. (1633/1999). *Discourse on method and meditations on first philosophy*. New York, NY: Hackett.

Descartes, R., and Voss, S. (1989). *The passions of the soul: An engl. transl. of Les passions de l'a^me*. Indianapolis u.a.: Hackett.

DiPaola, M., and Tschannen-Moran, M. 2001. Organizational citizenship behaviour in schools and its relationship to school climate. *Journal of School Leadership, 11,* 424–447.

Dolgin Katz, B. (2013). Book review: The handbook of transformative learning: Theory, research and practice. *Journal of Jewish Education, 79,* 453–457 (Jossey-Bass, San Francisco, CA, 2012). http://doi.org/10.1080/15244113.2013.844982

Drack, M. (n.d.). Ludwig von Bertalanffy's early system approach. Department of Theoretical Biology, University of Vienna, Retrieved from http://journals.isss.org/index.php/proceedings52nd/article/viewFile/1032/322

Duckworth, A. L., Peterson, C., Matthews, M. D., and Kelly, D. R. (2007). Grit: Perseverance and passion for long-term goals. *Journal of Personality and Social Psychology, 92*(6), 1087–1101. http://doi.org/10.1037/0022-3514.92.6.1087

Dweck, C. (1986). Motivational processes affecting learning. *American Psychologist, 41*(10), 1040–1048. http://dx.doi.org/10.1037/0003-066X.41.10.1040

Dweck, C. S. (1989). Motivation. In A. Lesgold and R. Glasers (Eds.), *Foundations for a psychology of education* (pp. 87–136). Hillsdale, NJ: Erlbaum.

Dweck, C. S. (2002). Beliefs that make smart people dumb. In R. J. Sternberg (Ed.), *Why smart people do stupid things*. New Haven, CT: Yale University Press.

Dweck, C. S. (2008). *Mindset: The new psychology of success*. New York, NY: Ballantine Books.

Dweck, C. S. (2010). Mind-sets and equitable education. *Principal Leadership, 10*(5), 26–29.

Dweck, C. S. (2012). Mindsets and human nature: Promoting change in the Middle East, the schoolyard, the racial divide, and willpower. *American Psychologist, 67*(8), 614. https://doi.org/10.1037/a0029783

Dweck, C. S. (2007). The secret to raising smart kids. *Scientific American Mind, 18*(6), 36–43. https://doi.org/10.1038/scientificamericanmind1207-36

Dweck, C. S. (2016). *Mindsets for the 21st century and beyond*. Washington, DC: Brookings Institution Press. Retrieved June 30, 2017 from https://www.brookings.edu/blog/education-plus-development/2016/06/06/mindsets-for-the-21st-century-and-beyond/

Dweck, C., Chiu, C., and Hong, Y. (1995). Implicit theories and their role in judgments and reactions: A world from two perspectives. *Psychological Inquiry, 6*(4), 267–285. https://doi.org/10.1207/s15327965pli0604_1

Dweck, C. S., and Leggett, E. L. (1988). A social-cognitive approach to motivation and personality. *Psychological Review, 95*(2), 256–273. https://doi.org/10.1037/0033-295X.95.2.256

Eagleman, D. (2015, March). Can we create new senses for humans? (Videofile). Retrieved from http://www.ted.com/talks/david_eagleman_can_we_create_new_senses_for_humans/transcript?language=en

Eisenberg, E. M. (2006). Karl Weick and the aesthetics of contingency. *Organization Studies, 27*(11), 1693–1707.

"Facts about Arnold" in FixQuotes.com. (n.d.) Retrieved May 26, 2017, from http://fixquotes.com/authors/arnold-h-glasgow.htm

Farrington, C. (2013, April 1). Academic mindsets as a critical component of deeper learning. Retrieved from http://www.hewlett.org/library/academic-mindsets-as-a-critical-component-of-deeper-learning/

Farrington, C., Roderick, M., Allensworth, E., Nagaoka, J., Seneca-Keyes, T., Johnson, D., and Beechum, N. (2012, June 1). University of Chicago Consortium on Chicago School Research. Retrieved December 8, 2014, from https://ccsr.uchicago.edu/sites/default/files/publications/Noncognitive Report.pdf#page=1&zoom=auto,582,813

Fischer, K. W. (1980). A theory of cognitive development: The control and construction of hierarchies of skills. *Psychological Review, 87*(6), 477–531. Retrieved from https://www.gse.harvard.edu/~ddl/articlesCopy/FischerTheoryCognDev1980.pdf

Fischer, K. W. (2006). Dynamic cycles of cognitive and brain development: Measuring growth in mind, brain, and education. In A. M. Battro and K. W. Fischer (Eds.), *The educated brain.* Cambridge, UK: Cambridge University Press. Retrieved September 2, 2016, from https://www.gse.harvard.edu/~ddl/articlesCopy/Fischer BrainCognDevtRefsRevFigs.0805.pdf

Fischer, K. W., and Rose, S. P. (1996). Dynamic growth cycles of brain and cognitive development. In R. Thatcher, G. R. Lyon, J. Rumsey, and N. Krasnegor (Eds.), *Developmental neuroimaging: Mapping the development of brain and behavior* (pp. 263–279). New York: Academic Press.

Fischer, K. W., and Yan, Z. (2002). Development of dynamic skill theory. In R. Lickliter and D. Lewkowicz (Eds.), *Conceptions of development: Lessons from the laboratory* (pp. 279–312). Hove, UK: Psychology Press.

Fisher, R., Ury, W., and Patton, B. (2011). *Getting to yes: Negotiating agreement without giving in.* New York: Penguin Books.

Fleeson, W. and Wilt, J. (2010). The relevance of Big Five trait content in behavior to subjective authenticity: Do high levels of within-person behavioral variability undermine or enable authenticity achievement? Journal of Personality, 78, 1353–1382.

Forsyth, J. K., Bachman, P., Mathalon, D. H., Roach, B. J., and Asarnow, R. F. (2015). Augmenting NMDA receptor signaling boosts experience-dependent neuroplasticity in the adult human brain. *Proceedings of the National Academy of Science (PNAS), 112,* 15331–15336.

Freitas, A. L., Gollwitzer, P., and Trope, Y. (2004). The influence of abstract and concrete mindsets on anticipating and guiding others' self-regulatory efforts. *Journal of Experimental Social Psychology, 40,* 739–752. https://doi.org/10.1016/j.jesp.2004.04.003

Garagnani, P., Pirazzini, C., Giuliani, C., Candela, M., Brigidi, P., Sevini, F., . . ., and Monti, D. (2014). The three genetics (nuclear DNA, mitochondrial DNA, and gut microbiome) of longevity in humans considered as metaorganisms. *BioMed Research International, 2014,*1–14. Article ID 560340, http://dx.doi.org/10.1155/2014/560340

Geys, B., and Murdoch, C. (2010). Measuring the "bridging" versus "bonding" nature of social networks: A proposal for integrating existing measures. *Sociology, 44*(3), 523–540. Retrieved November 11, 2016, from http://www.sagepub.co.uk/journals Permissions.nav

Gibson, M., Davey, B., and Cotton, N. (Directors) (2008). *Carrier*—Episode 7: "Rites of Passage," Chapter 4: "Swells" (Video file). United States. PBS documentary series. Retrieved from http://www.pbs.org/weta/carrier/full_episodes.htm

Gilbert, D. (2006, September). The surprising science of happiness (Video file). Retrieved from http://www.ted.com/talks/dan_gilbert_asks_why_are_we_happy/transcript?language=en

Gilbert, J. A., and Gilbert, J. (1995). Erratic–systematic–organic. *The TQM Magazine, 7*(2), 57–61.

Glattfelder, J. B. (2013, February). Who controls the world? (Video file). Retrieved from http://www.ted.com/talks/james_b_glattfelder_who_controls_the_world/transcript?language=en

Goddard, R. D. (2002). A theoretical and empirical analysis of the measurement of collective efficacy: The development of a short form. *Educational and Psychological Measurement, 93,* 467–476.

Gollwitzer, P. M. (1990). Action phases and mind-sets. In E. T. Higgins and R. M. Sorrentino (Eds.), *The handbook of motivation and cognition: Foundations of social behavior* (Vol. 2, pp. 53–92). New York: Guilford Press.

Guthrie, J. W., Garms, W. I., and Pierce, L. C. (1988). *School finance and education policy: Enhancing educational efficiency, equality, and choice* (2nd Ed.). Englewood Cliffs, NJ: Prentice Hall,

Hadhazy, A. (2010). Think twice: How the gut's "second brain" influences mood and well-being. *Scientific American.* Retrieved September 3, 2016, from http://www.scientificamerican.com/article/gut-second-brain/

Haimovitz, K., and Dweck, Carol, S. (2016). What predicts children's fixed and growth intelligence mind-sets? Not their parents' views of intelligence but their parents' views of failure. *Psychological Science, 27*(6), 859–869. http://doi.org/10.1177/0956797616639727

Hanson, J. L. (2015). Determination and validation of the "What's My School Mindset?" instrument factor structure (Order No. 3722197). Available from Dissertations and Theses at Montana State University; ProQuest Dissertations & Theses Global (1728126620). Retrieved from http://search.proquest.com/docview/17281 26620?accountid=28148

Hanson, J. L. (2017a). Determination and validation of the Project for Educational Research That Scales (PERTS) Survey factor structure. *Journal of Educational Issues, 3*(1), 64–82. http://doi.org/10.5296/jei.v3i1.10646

Hanson, J. (2017b). Testing the difference between school level and academic mind-set in the classroom: Implications for developing student psycho-social skills in secondary school classrooms. *Journal of Educational Issues, 3*(1), 44–63. http://doi.org/10.5296/jei.v3i1.10479

Hanson, J., Bangert, A., and Ruff, W. (2016). A validation study of the What's My School Mindset? Survey. *Journal of Educational Issues, 2*(2), 244–266. http://doi.org/10.5296/jei.v2i2.10138

Hanson, J., Loose, W., Reveles, U., and Hanshaw, G. (2017). Validation of the newly developed Graphical Inventory of Ethical Leadership (GIEL) Scale: Implications for administrator preparation and business leaders. *Journal of Educational Issues,* *3*(1), 19–43. http://doi.org/10.5296/jei.v3i1.10480

Hanson, J., Reveles, U., Loose, W., and Hanshaw, G. (2016, June 3). 3D leadership graphic inventory for school administrators (GISA). Conference Proceedings, Pacific Conference on Pre-K through K-12 Education 2016, http://www.thinksisu.org/event/education/#proceedings

Hanson, J., Ruff, W., and Bangert, A. (2016). Exploring the relationship between school growth mindset and organizational learning variables: Implications for multicultural education. *Journal of Educational Issues, 2*(2), 222–243. http://doi.org/10.5296/jei.v2i2.10075

Hari, J. (2015, July). Everything you think you know about addiction is wrong. (Video file). Retrieved from http://www.ted.com/talks/johann_hari_everything_you_think_you_know_about_addiction_is_wrong/transcript?language=en

Heartmath.com. (2016). About us. Heartmath. Retrieved from https://www.heart-math.com/about/

Helliwell, J. F., Huang, H., and Wang, S. (2014). Social capital and well-being in times of crisis. *Journal of Happiness Studies, 15,* 145–162. https://doi.org/10.1007/s10902-013-9441-z

Herrmann, M., and Brandstätter, V. (2015). Action crises and goal disengagement: Longitudinal evidence on the predictive validity of a motivational phase in goal striving. *Motivation Science, 1*(2), 121–136. https://doi.org/10.1037/mot0000016

Herzog, W. (Director) (2007). *Encounters at the End of the World* (Film). Antarctic Artists and Writers Program of National Science Foundation's Office of Polar Programs.

Heslin, P., VandeWalle, D., and Latham, G. (2007). Engagement in employee coaching: The role of managers' implicit person theory. *Personnel psychology, 42*(4), 268–270. https://doi.org/10.1080/00050060701648209

Heyman, G. D., and Dweck, C. S. (1998). Children's thinking about traits: Implications for judgments of the self and others. *Child Development, 64*(2), 391–403. https://doi.org/10.1111/j.1467-8624.1998.tb06197.x

"History of Glass Manufacture" (2012). In *Encyclopaedia Britannica,* (11th Ed. Vol. 12). Retrieved from http://www.gutenberg.org/files/38539/38539-8.txt

"Hypnosis and mental structure," (n.d.). Retrieved February 13, 2017, from http://webcache.googleusercontent.com/search?q=cache:k0JgxDybEaUJ:www.sharp-printinginc.com/911/index.php%3Fmodule%3Dpagemaster%26PAGE_user_op%3Dview_printable%26PAGE_id%3D297%26lay_quiet%3D1+&cd=1&hl=en&ct=clnk&gl=us

Hofstede, G. (2001). *Cultured consequences* (2nd Ed.). Thousand Oaks, CA: Sage.

Hong, Y., Chiu, C., Dweck, C., Lin, D., and Wan, W. (1999). Implicit theories, attributions, and coping: A meaning system approach. *Journal of Personality and Social Psychology, 77*(3), 588–599. https://doi.org/10.1037/0022-3514.77.3.588

Hong, Y. Y., Chiu, C. Y., Dweck, C. S., and Sacks, R. (1997). Implicit theories and evaluative processes in person cognition. *Journal of Experimental Social Psychology, 33,* 296–323. https://doi.org/10.1006/jesp.1996.1324

Hoy, W., Tarter, C., and Kottkamp, B. (1991). *Open schools/healthy schools measuring organizational climate.* Newbury Park, NY: Sage Publications.

Jensen, J., Rustad, P. I., Kolnes, A. J., and Lai, Y. (2011). The role of skeletal muscle glycogen breakdown for regulation of insulin sensitivity by exercise. *Frontiers in Physiology, 2,* 112. https://doi.org/10.3389/fphys.2011.00112

Job, V., Bernecker, K., and Dweck, C. S. (2012). Are implicit motives the need to feel certain affect? Motive-affect congruence predicts relationship satisfaction. *Personality and Social Psychology Bulletin, 38*(12), 1552–1565. https://doi.org/10.1177/0146167212454920

Jozefowiez, J. (2014). The many faces of Pavlovian conditioning. *International Journal of Comparative Psychology, 27*(4) 526–536. http://escholarship.org/uc/item/0bg0b3kq

Kahneman, D. (2011). *Thinking, fast and slow.* New York, NY: Farrar, Straus and Giroux.

Kalshoven, K., Den Hartog, D. N., and De Hoogh, A. H. B. (2011). Ethical leadership at work questionnaire (ELW): Development and validation of a multidimensional measure. *The Leadership Quarterly, 22*(1), 51–69. https://doi.org/10.1016/j.leaqua.2010.12.007

Kang, S., Scharmann, L., and Noh, T. (2004). Reexamining the role of cognitive conflict in science concept learning. *Research in Science Education, 34,* 71–96 and 91. https://doi.org/10.1023/B:RISE.0000021001.77568.b3

Katz, B. D. (2013). Book Reviews. Edward W. Taylor and Patricia Cranton and Associates, The handbook of transformative learning: Theory, research and practice. *Journal of Jewish Education, 79*(4), 453–457. http://doi.org/10.1080/15244113.2013.844982

King, M. L., Jr. (1965, June). *Remaining awake through a great revolution.* Commencement Address for Oberlin College. Oberlin College, Oberlin, OH. Retrieved November 21, 2016, from http://www.oberlin.edu/external/EOG/BlackHistory Month/MLK/CommAddress.html

King, P., and Kitchener, K. (1994). *Developing reflective judgment: Understanding and promoting intellectual growth and critical thinking in adolescents and adults.* San Francisco, CA: Jossey-Bass.

King, P. M., and Shuford, B. C. (1996). A multicultural view is a more cognitively complex view: Cognitive development and multicultural education. *American Behavioral Scientist, 40,* 153. https://doi.org/10.1177/0002764296040002006

Kirshner, D., and Whitson. J. A. (1998). Obstacles to understanding learning as situated. *Educational Researcher, 27*(8), 22–28. https://doi.org/10.3102/0013189X027008022

Korac-Kakabadse, N., Korac-Kakabadse, A., and Kouzmin, A. (2001). Leadership renewal: Toward a philosophy of wisdom. *International Review of Administrative Sciences, 67,* 207–227. https://doi.org/10.1177/0020852301672002

Kouzes, J. M., and Posner, B. Z. (2007). *Leadership challenge* (4th Ed.). San Francisco, CA: Jossey-Bass.

Krucoff, C. (1984, January 29). The 6 o'clock scholar. *The Washington Post,* Retrieved from https://www.washingtonpost.com/archive/lifestyle/1984/01/29/the-6-oclock-scholar/eed58de4-2dcb-47d2-8947-b0817a18d8fe/?utm_term=.5fb6240a2dc8

Krull, D. S., Loy, M. H., Lin, J., Wang, C., Chen, S., and Zhao, X. (1999). The fundamental attribution error: Correspondence bias in individualistic and collectivist cultures. *Personality and Social Psychology Journal, 25*(10), 1208–1219. https://doi.org/10.1177/0146167299258003

Lane, A. (Ed.). (2007). *Mood and human performance: Conceptual, measurement, and applied issues*. New York, NY: Nova Science Publishers, Inc.

Lawton, A., and Páez, I. (2014). Developing a framework for ethical leadership. *Journal of Business Ethics, 130*(3), 639–649. https://doi.org/10.1007/s10551-014-2244-2

Lee, K. (2016, May). Can you really tell if a kid is lying? (Video file). Retrieved February 14, 2017, from https://www.ted.com/talks/kang_lee_can_you_really_tell_if_a_kid_is_lying/transcript?language=en

Lewis, C. S. (2002). *The complete C.S. Lewis Signature classics*. San Francisco, CA: Harper Collins. Retrieved December 29, 2016, from http://www.goodreads.com/quotes/64682-hell-is-a-state-of-mind---ye-never-said

Lewis, D. (1969). *Convention: A philosophical study*. Cambridge, MA: Harvard University Press.

Lloyd-Price, J., Abu-Ali, G., and Huttenhower, C. (2016). The healthy human microbiome. *Genome Medicine, 8*(51), 2–11. http://doi.org/10.1186/s13073-016-0307-y

Lönnqvist, J. E., Verkasalo, M., Wichardt, P. C., and Walkowitz, G. (2013). Personal values and prosocial behaviour in strategic interactions: Distinguishing value-expressive from value-ambivalent behaviours. *European Journal of Social Psychology, 43*(6), 554–569. http://doi.org/10.1002/ejsp.1976

Ma, X. (2003). Sense of belonging to school: Can schools make a difference? *Journal of Educational Research, 96*(6), 1–9. https://doi.org/10.1080/00220670309596617

MacIver, R. M. (1917). *Community, a sociological study*. London, UK: Macmillan and Co.

MacIver, R. M. (1949). *The elements of social science* (9th Ed.). London, UK: Methuen and Company.

Malle, B. F. (2011). Attribution theories: How people make sense of behavior. *Theories in Social Psychology, 2011,* 72–95.

Markus, H. R., and Kitayama, S. (1991). Culture and the self: Implications for cognition, emotion, and motivation. *Psychological Review, 98*(2), 224–253. https://doi.org/10.1037/0033-295X.98.2.224

Marsden, M. (2003). Kaitiakitanga: A definitive introduction to the holistic worldview of the Māori. In T. E. C. Royal (Ed.), *The woven universe: Selected writings of Rev. Māori Marsden* (pp. 54-72). Otaki, New Zealand: Estate of Reverend Marsden.

Marsden, M., and Henare, T. A. (1992). Kaitiakitanga: A definitive introduction to the holistic world view of the Māori. Unpublished manuscript. Retrieved from http://www.marinenz.org.nz/documents/Marsden_1992_Kaitiakitanga.pdf.

Marsh, A. (September, 2016). Why some people are more altruistic than others (Video file). Retrieved from https://www.ted.com/talks/abigail_marsh_why_some_people_are_more_altruistic_than_others/transcript?language=en

Mascret, N., Roussel, P., and Cury, F. (2015). Using implicit measures to highlight science teachers' implicit theories of intelligence. *European Journal of Psychology of Education, 30*(3), 269–280. https://doi.org/10.1007/s10212-015-0249-6

Maslow, A. H. (1954). *Motivation and personality*. New York, NY: Harper & Row.

McDonald, K. (Director) (2016). *Sky ladder: The art of Cai Guo-Quiang* (Film). China.

McGonigal, K. (2013, June). How to make stress your friend (Video file). Retrieved from https://www.ted.com/talks/kelly_mcgonigal_how_to_make_stress_your_friend/transcript?language=en

Mezirow, J., and Dirkx, J. (2006). Musings and Reflections on the Meaning, Context and Process of Transformative Learning. *Journal of Transformative Education, 4*(2), 123–139. https://doi.org/10.1177/1541344606287503

Midgley, C., Maehr, M. L., Hruda, L. Z., Anderman, E., Anderman, L., Freeman, K. E., . . . and Urdan, T. (2000). Manual for the patterns of adaptive learning scales. Ann Arbor, 1001, 48109-1259. Retrieved June 29, 2017 from "http://www.umich.edu/~pals/PALS%202000_V13Word97.pdf" www.umich.edu/~pals/PALS%202000_V13Word97.pdf

Milgram, N. A. (1986). *Stress and coping in time of war: Generalizations from the Israeli experience* (Psychosocial Stress Series). New York, NY: Brunner/Mazel.

Milgram, S. (1974). *Obedience to authority: An experimental view.* New York, NY: Harper & Row.

Mintzberg, H. (1983). *Power in and around organizations.* Englewood Cliffs, NJ: Prentice-Hall.

Moser, J. S., Schroder, H. S., Heeter, C., Moran, T. P., and Lee, Y. H. (2011). Mind your errors evidence for a neural mechanism linking growth mind-set to adaptive posterror adjustments. *Psychological Science, 22*(12), Retrieved from http://journals.sagepub.com/doi/abs/10.1177/0956797611419520

Mridha, D. (2017). Debasish Mridha > Quotes > Quotable Quote. *Goodreads.* Retrieved from http://www.goodreads.com/quotes/7510923-the-measure-of-a-person-s-strength-is-not-his-muscular

Murphy, M., and Dweck, C. (2010). A culture of genius: How an organization's lay theory shapes people's cognition, affect, and behavior. *Personality and Social Psychology Bulletin, 36*(3), 283–296. https://doi.org/10.1177/0146167209347380

Nardi, C, Wozner, Y., and Margalit, C. (1986). Behavioral group treatment. In N. A. Milgram (Ed.), *Stress and coping in time of war.* New York: Brunner/Mazel, Inc.

Ng, T. W. H., Sorensen, K. L., and Eby, L. T. (2006). Locus of control at work: A meta-analysis. *Journal of Organizational Behavior, 27*(8), 1057–1087. https://doi.org/10.1002/job.416

Nidditch, P. (Ed.). (1979). *John Locke: An essay concerning human understanding.* New York, NY: Oxford University Press.

Niqab, M., Hanson, J., Bangert, A., Kannan, S., Sharma, S., and Ghaffar, A. (In process). Measuring organizational citizenship behaviors: A tool for developing self-improvement processes and a comparison with growth mindset cultures in schools.

Nixon, B. (Director) (2014). *Mission blue* (Film). United States. Living Oceans Production.

Nouwen, H. (2017). Nouwen quotes. Retrieved March 4, 2017, from https://www.goodreads.com/author/quotes/4837.Henri_J_M_Nouwen

Novak, J. (2002). Meaningful learning: The essential factor for conceptual change in limited or inappropriate propositional hierarchies leading to empowerment of learners. *Science Education, 86*(4), 548–571. http://doi.org/10.1002/sce.10032.

Novak, J., and Gowin, D. (1984). *Learning how to learn*. Cambridge, UK: Cambridge University Press.

O'Hanlon, B. (1994). The third wave. Family Therapy Networker, November/December, 1994, pp. 19–29. "Comment on 'Manners Matter,' (case example)," *The Family Therapy Networker, 21*(4), 81–83, July/August 1997.

O'Leary, V. E. (1998). Strength in the face of adversity: Individual and social thriving. *Journal of Social Issues, 54*(2), 425–446. https://doi.org/10.1111/j.1540-4560.1998.tb01228.x

Ogden, J. (2003). Some problems with social cognition models: A pragmatic and conceptual analysis. *Health Psychology, 22*(4), 424–428. https://doi.org/10.1037/0278-6133.22.4.424

Page, K. M., and Vella-Brodrick, D. A. (2008). The "what" and "how" of employee well-being: A new model. *Social Indicators Research Journal, 90,* 441–458. https://doi.org/10.1007/s11205-008-9270-3

Paine, T. (1792). *The rights of man (Part II)*. Retrieved December 31, 2016, from https://www.gutenberg.org/files/3742/3742-h/3742-h.htm

Park, G., and Thayer, J. (2014). From the heart to the mind: Cardiac vagal tone modulates top-down and bottom-up visual perception and attention to emotional stimuli. *Frontiers in Psychology, 5*(278), 1–8. https://doi.org/10.3389/fpsyg.2014.00278

Parks, L., and Guay, R. (2012). Can personal values predict performance? Evidence in an academic setting. *Applied Psychology, 6*(1), 149–173. http://doi.org/10.1111/j.1464-0597.2011.00461.x

Pearson, G. (2011). African famine: "I See You." *The Huffington Post*. Retrieved November 21, 2016, from http://www.huffingtonpost.ca/glen-pearson/africa-famine_b_922063.html

Peralta, N. Á. (2013). Ownership control, transnational corporations and financial power. Retrieved from https://mappingignorance.org/2013/05/14/ownership-control-transnational-corporations-and-financial-power/

Perry, B. L. (2004). Evaluation and assessment of the effects of adversity on organizational leadership. Dissertation submitted to Brigham Young University, UMI 3148998.

PERTS. (2016a). Academic Mindsets Assessment. Retrieved June 1, 2017, from https://mindsetmeter.appspot.com/share/dlmooc

PERTS. (2016b). Our Mission. Retrieved June 1, 2017 from https://www.perts.net/about

Petit, P. (2014). *Creativity: The perfect crime*. New York: Riverhead Books.

Piaget, J. (1958). The growth of logical thinking from childhood to adolescence. *AMC, 10,* 12.

Pink, D. (2009, August). The puzzle of motivation? (Video file). Retrieved from https://www.ted.com/talks/dan_pink_on_motivation

Plaks, J. E., Grant, H., and Dweck, C. S. (2005). Violations of implicit theories and the sense of prediction and control: Implications for motivated person perception. *Journal of Personality and Social Psychology, 88*(2), 245–262. https://doi.org/10.1037/0022-3514.88.2.245

Ponton, M. K., and Rhea, N. R. (2006). Autonomous learning from a social cognitive perspective. *New Horizons in Adult Education and Human Resource Development, 20*(2), 38–49. https://doi.org/10.1002/nha3.10250

Poplin, M., & Weeres, J. (1994). Voices from the inside: A report on schooling from inside the classroom. Claremont, CA: Institute for Education in Transformation at the Claremont Graduate School.

Power, P., Barnes-Holmes, D., Barnes-Holmes, Y., and Stewart, I. (2009). The implicit relational assessment procedure (IRAP) as a measure of implicit relative preferences: A first study. *The Psychological Record, 59,* 621–640. Retrieved October 13, 2016, from http://opensiuc.lib.siu.edu/cgi/viewcontent.cgi?article=1040& context=tpr

Rawls, J. (1985). Justice as Fairness: Political Not Metaphysical. *Philosophy and Public Affairs, 14*(3), 223–251. Retrieved from http://www.jstor.org/stable/2265349.

Reed, L. L., Vidaver-Cohen, D., and Colwell, S. R. (2011). A new scale to measure executive servant leadership: Development, analysis, and implications for research. *Journal of Business Ethics, 101*(3), 415–434. https://doi.org/10.1007/s10551-010-0729-1

Rejcek, P. (2012). Evolutionary insight: New harbor and forams may offer window into explosion of multicellular life a half-billion years ago. United States Antarctic Program. *The Antarctic Sun.* Retrieved October 18, 2016, from https://antarcticsun. usap.gov/science/contenthandler.cfm?id=2639

Roberts, M. (1998). Indigenous knowledge and Western science: Perspectives from the Pacific. In D. Hodson (Ed.), *Science and technology education and ethnicity: An Aotearoa/New Zealand perspective* (pp. 59–75). Wellington, New Zealand: The Royal Society of New Zealand.

Rock, D., Siegel, D. J., Poelmans, S. A., and Payne, J. (2012). The healthy mind platter. *NeuroLeadership Journal, 4,* 1–23. Retrieved November 21, 2016, from http:// davidrock.net/files/02_The_Healthy_Mind_Platter_US.pdf

Rossi, E. L., and Cheek, D. B. (1994). *Mind-body therapy: Methods of ideodynamic healing in hypnosis.* New York: W.W. Norton.

Round, K. (Director) (2015). The divide (Dartmouth Films). United Kingdom.

Rowland, N. D. (2014, April 4). "It is easier to build strong children than to repair broken men" (Frederick Douglass, 1817–1895) (Web blog post). Retrieved from https://drandrewrowland.wordpress.com/2014/04/25/it-is-easier-to-build-strong-children-than-to-repair-broken-men-frederick-douglass-1817-1895/

Ruff, W. (2002). Constructing the role of instructional leader: The mental models of urban elementary school principals. (Doctoral dissertation). The University of Texas at San Antonio.

Schwartz, S. H. (1992). Universals in the content and structure of values: Theory and empirical tests in 20 countries. In M. Zanna (Ed.), *Advances in experimental social psychology* (Vol. 25, pp. 1–65). New York: Academic Press.

The science behind the smile. (2012, January–February). Retrieved from https://hbr. org/2012/01/the-science-behind-the-smile

Senge, P. (2000). Schools that learn: A fifth discipline fieldbook for educators, parents, and everyone who cares about education. New York: Doubleday.

Senge, P. (2009, November 30). What the vision does. Awaken.org. Retrieved December 31, 2016, from http://www.awakin.org/read/view.php?tid=669

Senge, P. M. (1990, revised 2006). *The fifth discipline: The art & practice of the learning organization.* New York, NY: Doubleday.

Shenk, J. W. (2009). What makes us happy? *The Atlantic.* Retrieved from https://www.theatlantic.com/magazine/archive/2009/06/what-makes-us-happy/307439/

Sherman, D. K., and Cohen, G. L. (2006). The psychology of self-defense: Self-affirmation theory. In M. P. Zanna (Ed.), *Advances in experimental social psychology* (Vol. 38, pp. 183–242). San Diego, CA: Academic Press. https://doi.org/10.1016/S0065-2601(06)38004-5

Shermer, M. (2007). *Why Darwin matters: The case against intelligent design.* Holt Paperbacks. Why Darwin Matters Quotes, Goodreads. Retrieved from https://www.goodreads.com/work/quotes/1630970-why-darwin-matters-the-case-against-intelligent-design

Sinha, P. (2010, February). How brains learn to see. (Video file). Retrieved from https://www.ted.com/talks/pawan_sinha_on_how_brains_learn_to_see/transcript?language=en

Spector, P. E. (1988). Development of the work locus of control scale. *Journal of Occupational Psychology, 61,* 335–340. https://doi.org/10.1111/j.2044-8325.1988.tb00470.x

Spector, P. E., Cooper, C. L., Sanchez, J. I., O'Driscoll, M., Sparks, K., Bernin, P., Büssing, A., Dewe, P., Hart, P., Lu, L., Miller, K., de Moraes, L. F. R., Ostrognay, G. M., Pagon, M., Pitariu, H., Poelmans, S., Radhakrishnan, P., Russinova, V., Salamatov, V., Salgado, J., Shima, S., Siu, O. L., Stora, J. B., Teichmann, M., Theorell, T., Vlerick, P., Westman, M., Widerszal-Bazyl, M., Wong, P., and Yu, S. (2001). Do national levels of individualism and internal locus of control relate to well-being: An ecological level international study? *Journal of Organizational Behavior, 22,* 815–832. https://doi.org/10.1002/job.118

Steele, C. M., and Liu, T. J. (1983). Dissonance processes as self-affirmation. *Journal of Personality and Social Psychology, 45,* 5–19. https://doi.org/10.1037/0022-3514.45.1.5

Sternberg, R. J. (1985a). *Beyond IQ: A triarchic theory of human intelligence.* Cambridge, UK: Cambridge University Press.

Sternberg, R. J. (1985b). Human intelligence: The model is the message. *Science, 23,* 1111–1118. https://doi.org/10.1126/science.230.4730.1111

Sternberg, R. J. (2005). The theory of successful intelligence. *Journal of Psychology, 39*(2), 189–202.

Sternberg, R. J., and Detterman, D. K. (Eds.). (1986). *What is intelligence?* Norwood, NJ: Ablex.

Stewart, G. M. (2007). *Kaupapa Māori science* (Thesis, Doctor of Philosophy [PhD]). The University of Waikato. Retrieved from http://hdl.handle.net/10289/2598

Strogatz, S. (2004, February). The science of sync. Retrieved from http://www.ted.com/talks/steven_strogatz_on_sync?language=en

Surel, D. (2014). Thinking from the heart: Heart brain science. Noetic Systems International. Retrieved from http://noeticsi.com/thinking-from-the-heart-heart-brain-science/

Tarter, C., and Hoy, W. (2004). A systems approach to quality in elementary schools: A theoretical and empirical analysis. *Journal of Educational Administration, 42*(5), 539–554. https://doi.org/10.1108/09578230410554052

Thomas, F. and Johnston, O. (1995). *The illusion of life: Disney animation.* New York, NY: Walt Disney Productions.

Thornton, L., and McEntee, M. E. (1995). Learner centered schools as a mindset, and the connection with mindfulness and multiculturalism. *Theory into Practice, 34*(4), 250–257. https://doi.org/10.1080/00405849509543688

Tobgay, L. T. (2016). Keynote address by the honourable prime minister of Bhutan, Lyonchoen Tshering Tobgay, to the International Conference on Gross National Happiness. The Centre for Bhutan Studies and GNH Research. Retrieved September 2, 2016, from http://www.grossnationalhappiness.com/2015GNHConference/HPMSpeech_2015GNHConference.pdf

Tourangeau, R., Rasinski, K. A., Bradburn, N., and D'andrade, R. (1989). Belief accessibility and context effects in attitude measurement. *Journal of Experimental Social Psychology, 25*(5), 401–421. https://doi.org/10.1016/0022-1031(89)90030-9

Tversky, A., and Kahneman, D. (1974). Judgment under uncertainty: Heuristics and biases. *Science, 185*(4157), 1124–1131. https://doi.org/10.1126/science.185.4157.1124

Tyson, N. D. (2015, November 18). What science is—and how and why it works (Web blog post). Retrieved from http://www.huffingtonpost.com/neil-degrasse-tyson/what-science-is-and-how-and-why-it-works_b_8595642.html

Vella, J. (2002). Quantum learning: Teaching as dialogue (Chapter 7). *New Directions for Adult & Continuing Education, 93,* 73–83. https://doi.org/10.1002/ace.51

Vitali, S., Glattfelder, J. B., and Battiston, S. (2011). The network of global corporate control. *PloS One, 6*(10), e25995. https://doi.org/10.1371/journal.pone.0025995

von Bertalanffy, L. (1968). *General system theory: Foundations, development, applications.* New York, NY: George Brazille.

Vucinic, S. (2005, July). Why we should invest in a free press (Video file). Retrieved from http://www.ted.com/talks/sasa_vucinic_invests_in_free_press/transcript?language=en

Wales, J. (2006, August). The birth of Wikipedia (Video file). Retrieved from https://www.ted.com/talks/jimmy_wales_on_the_birth_of_wikipedia/transcript?language=en

Walton, G. M. (2014). The new science of wise psychological interventions. *Current Directions in Psychological Science, 23*(1), 73–82. https://doi.org/10.1177/0963721413512856

Wang, Q., Bowling, N. A., and Eschleman, K. J. (2010). A meta-analytic examination of work and general locus of control. *Journal of Applied Psychology, 95,* 61–768. https://doi.org/10.1037/a0017707

Weschler, D. (1943). Non-intellective factors in general intelligence. *Journal of Abnormal and Social Psychology, 38*(1), 101–103. https://doi.org/10.1037/h0060613

Whyte, D. (2013). Gratitude. November Thoughts. Facebook. Retrieved November 26, 2016, from https://www.facebook.com/213407562018588/photos/a.2134443153 48246.68208.213407562018588/784861051539900/

Williams, S. R., and Ivey, K. M. C. (2001). Affective assessment and mathematics classroom engagement: A case study. *Educational Studies in Mathematics, 47,* 75–100. https://doi.org/10.1023/A:1017987500929

Wilms, W. W., Hardcastle, A. J., and Zell, D. M. (1994). Cultural transformation at NUMMI. *Sloan Management Review, 36*(1), 99.

Wilson, H. V. (1907). On some phenomena of coalescence and regeneration in sponges. *Journal of Experimental Zoology, 2,* 245–258. https://doi.org/10.1002/jez.1400050204

Woike, B. A. (2008). The state of the story in personality psychology. *Social and Personality Psychology Compass, 2*(1), 434–443. https://doi.org/10.1111/j.1751-9004.2007.00070.x

Wolpert, D. M., Diedrichsen, J., and Flanagan, J. R. (2011). Principles of sensorimotor learning. *Nature Reviews Neuroscience, 12*(12), 739–751. https://doi.org/10.1038/nrn3112

Yeager, D. S., Johnson, R., Spitzer, B. J., Trzesniewski, K. H., Powers, J., and Dweck, C. S. (2014). The far-reaching effects of believing people can change: Implicit theories of personality shape stress, health, and achievement during adolescence. *Journal of Personality and Social Psychology, 106*(6), 867–884. https://doi.org/10.1037/a0036335

Yeo, R. (2005). Revisiting the roots of learning organization: A synthesis of the learning organization literature. *The Learning Organization, 12*(4), 368–382. https://doi.org/10.1108/09696470510599145

Yin, R. K. (2014) *Case study research: Design and methods* (5th Ed.). Los Angeles, CA: Sage.

Young, H. P. (2008). Social norms. In Steven N. Durlauf and Lawrence E. Blume (Eds.), *The New Palgrave Dictionary of Economics* (2nd Ed.). Palgrave Macmillan. Retrieved from *The New Palgrave Dictionary of Economics Online*. Palgrave Macmillan. November 19, 2016. http://doi.org/10.1057/9780230226203.1563

Yukl, G., Mahsud, R., Hassan, S., and Prussia, G. E. (2013). An improved measure of ethical leadership. *Journal of Leadership and Organizational Studies, 20*(1), 38–48. https://doi.org/10.1177/1548051811429352

Zittrain, J. (2009, September). The web as random acts of kindness (Video file). Retrieved from https://www.ted.com/talks/jonathan_zittrain_the_web_is_a_random_act_of_kindness/transcript?language=en

Index

About the Author

Janet Hanson has a broad background in business, education, and leadership. She earned her bachelor of arts in business administration: accounting, from California State University, Fullerton, and then worked as an auditor for Price Waterhouse and Company.

Janet's broad experience includes raising three children on a small farm in the northwestern United States. Her interest in education began with home schooling and then branched into public education when her oldest son entered public middle school. She earned her master's in education: curriculum and instruction through Azusa Pacific University and qualified for a multiple subject teaching credential, high school standard math credential, and administrator credential. She served as a teacher, private junior high and high school administrator, and superintendent for a K-12 public school district.

Throughout her career, Janet has woven the use of technology into the educational curriculum. Her first project included winning a national grant from Toshiba Corporation, in 2004, with which she supervised multiple projects for integrating the use of the Internet and laptops in elementary, high school, and community library programs.

Janet earned her doctorate in education, at Montana State University, Bozeman, while working as a graduate research assistant in the Department of Educational Leadership. She explored psychosocial features of learning, such as mindset, and worked on projects in multicultural education and developing trainings for school board trustees and legislators. Her research has included the validation and determination of the factors of the school-level growth mindset survey, *What's My School Mindset*, developed by Mindset Works, Inc., and the classroom academic mindset Project for Educational Research That Scale (PERTS) survey provided for use on their websites.

Janet has presented, authored, and coauthored on growth mindset, academic mindset, a newly developed ethical leadership survey, organizational learning variables, implications for multicultural education, a newly developed organizational citizenship behavior survey, and micro-learning for leadership professional development on the job including multimedia and social networking media.

Janet is assistant professor at Azusa Pacific University, teaching and supervising candidates for administrative services credentials, and students in the master's and doctoral programs. She serves on the Institutional Review Board committee for reviewing research proposals to ensure Human Subject Rights.